You can be...

A Radiant Character

Published in Perth, Australia
by Cypress Project

Cypress
Project

www.cypressproject.com.au

NKJV. Unless otherwise noted, Scriptures are taken from the NEW KING JAMES VERSION®. Copyright© 1982 by Thomas Nelson, Inc. Used by permission. All rights reserved.

NLT. Scriptures marked NLT are taken from the HOLY BIBLE, NEW LIVING TRANSLATION, Copyright© 1996, 2004, 2007 by Tyndale House Foundation. Used by permission of Tyndale House Publishers, Inc., Carol Stream, Illinois 60188. All rights reserved. Used by permission.

GNB. Scriptures and additional materials quoted are from the Good News Bible © 1994 published by the Bible Societies/HarperCollins Publishers Ltd UK, Good News Bible© American Bible Society 1966, 1971, 1976, 1992. Used with permission.

International Standard Book Number (ISBN)
978-0-9804172-3-4

A catalogue record for this
book is available from the
NATIONAL
LIBRARY   National Library of Australia
OF AUSTRALIA

Contents

Dedication

This book is dedicated to

My wonderful wife Delcie,
who for nearly 48 years has been
a true friend, encourager and partner in ministry,
and
our sons Andrew and John and their families
from whom I have learned so much.

Foreword

I have known Dr Don Hardgrave as a close friend for almost 50 years, and have enjoyed a warm and cordial working relationship with him throughout that time. No one of my acquaintance is more passionate about the importance of properly understanding the Wesleyan doctrine of holiness and giving expression to it in one's everyday life. Don firmly believes that the Christian church is most truly a community of light in this darkening age when God's people radiate Christ's character, both in public and in private. I know of no one on the Australian scene who is more qualified or better equipped to write a work of this kind.

Raised in Brisbane, Don spent four years as a teacher in Queensland State primary and high schools before responding to God's call to train for the ministry. A graduate of Melbourne Bible Institute and of Kings Theological College, he has actively participated in the planting and 'repotting' of many churches since 1972. He obtained his MA in Church Health in 1982, and Doctor of Biblical Studies in 1989.

Soon after joining the Wesleyan Methodist Church in 1974, Don was appointed National Secretary for Church Extension and Evangelism—a role that afforded him opportunity to exercise his considerable aptitude and passion for commending the gospel to the unchurched, and in many cases linking together Christians who were eager to hear the message of scriptural holiness presented in a fresh, winsome and compelling way. His ministry in this role and his later ministry as Superintendent laid a solid foundation for ongoing growth and impact, especially in communities where local Wesleyan Methodist churches were planted.

As well as pastoral ministry, he has especially enjoyed—and showed remarkable giftedness for—camp ministry to high-schoolers and young adults since 1968, reaching over 15,000 teens, many of whom came to Christ. Some of these have gone on to full-time Christian service. Two features of Don's ministry to campers stand out i) small-group studies conducted by competent and dedicated team leaders (of whom I was privileged to be one), and ii) a strong discipleship emphasis that engages both heart and mind in the quest for a disciplined, joyful and effective Christian life. As a serious student of church history, he has done special research on John Wesley's small-group meetings in eighteenth-century England. The insights gained from this study have been used in strengthening the small-group life in many local churches and in preserving the fruits of spiritual growth through personal accountability.

More recently he has served parishes as an interim pastor in Baptist churches in Innisfail, Tully, Whitsunday, Bowen and Mackay Beaches, with encouraging results. In keeping with the Master's mandate (Matthew 28:19), Don's passion is making disciples, and his resources have been used extensively in Australia and overseas, with significant response in the lives of those who participated. Other ministries include speaking at Promise Keepers and Keswick conventions. Like the apostle Paul, Don freely acknowledges that all to whom the treasure of the gospel is entrusted are "like common clay pots, in order to show that the supreme power belongs to God, not to us" (2 Corinthians 4: 7 GNB).

Don is the author of several books, including serving as editor of a songbook in today's English. He was guest-lecturer at theological seminaries in Switzerland and the USA during his long-service leave in 1995-6, and more recently at the Brisbane School of Theology (formerly BCQ). He is currently providing training in Brisbane and in Queensland regional centres under the CALAM program for the Baptists and the Wesleyans.

The book before you is the fruit of long, careful biblical study and sustained reflection on the lives of godly men and women whose testimonies God has blessed through the ages. It also contains the insights Don himself has gained in his own earnest quest for "[the] holiness without which no one will see the Lord" (Hebrews 12:14). I confidently predict that the reading of this book will provide "a word in season" to those who are weary of living a sub-standard Christian life, and are longing to radiate Christ's matchless character in their world.

Rev. Peter Howe

Introduction

When Japanese motor-vehicle manufacturers were expanding their exports to the west, a Tokyo car-hire firm had the following instructions for its English customers: "When passenger of foot heave in sight, tootle the horn. Trumpet him melodiously at first, but if he still obstacle your passage, then tootle him with vigor. If honorable horse obstacle your path, pull over until he pass away."[1] The Japanese English made some kind of sense and we got the message, but with effort. My hope is that this resource will be easy to read and encouraging to apply.

There is more to the Christian life than simply becoming a believer. There is abundant evidence that God can and does meet people who will give themselves completely to His will and plan. This unfolds an adventure for their earthly journey which is both challenging and satisfying. The purpose of this book is to unpack that. We will consider the lives of some outstanding men and women who made a difference in many parts of the world and eras of history. Then we will identify a common strand which was a vital part of their destiny.

My years of ministry to local congregations, conferences and camps have been a great privilege. God has been wonderfully faithful all along the way. The message at the heart of this book was absolutely essential to the remarkable success He gave in all those years, as changed people made an impact on those around them.

Dr Will Sangster, a British pastor, comments:

Every normal person would like to be a radiant personality: to be respected, attractive and, indeed, loved: to be at peace within, useful, happy and sought after—not just for the things they might be able to give, but for themselves alone.... in happy and easy relations with others, and to anybody possessing this inner treasure something else is added: an outward sparkle on their personality or (at least) the glow of a

---

[1] Alister E. McGrath, *The Future of Christianity* (Oxford, UK: Blackwell Publishers Ltd., 2002), 26.

1

quiet joy.... But how does one get it? What is the way to radiant personality?[2]

The experience of what we call 'conversion' often comes at the end of a time of restlessness and searching for the meaning and purpose of life, followed by the discovery that it is only to be found in a relationship with Jesus, God's Son. The weeks following include the painful discovery that, while we are grateful to be freed from the guilt of past sins, and pleased to have a friendship with the Lord, there is still a part of us that really wants to run our own lives. That issue is the main subject of this book, along with what can be done about it. My prayer is that you will discover how to complete what began at conversion, so your life will be very fulfilling and satisfied. If you have never made such a commitment, the contents of this little volume will at least give you a clearer picture of the wonderful possibility that is available to you.

As a hiker, I know what it is to find a creek bed that is dry when you had been looking forward to cool fresh water—always a disappointment. Dry, empty Christians are likewise a disappointment to themselves, to others, and to God. But when our hearts are filled with the Holy Spirit and we grow under His guidance, those things that were displeasing to God are replaced by new ways and our whole character changes. We become a stream of *living* water.

This is not a book on how to pray, though prayer is foundational to everything that is included. Neither is it a book defending the Bible. Spurgeon, the great English pastor, once said, "You don't defend a lion from attack, you let it loose." I believe the scriptures are inspired, infallible and inerrant from cover to cover. There is plenty of evidence for their reliability and dynamic impact on people individually, and on nations as a whole. Hence, we will refer to the Bible often.

I should add that this book has not addressed evangelism, or the evidence for the truth of our beliefs, important as that is. Sharing expands our faith and is *vital* for the sake of others as well. When God's love is flowing through us, it authenticates our testimony so that some people will be asking themselves, "What makes this person different?" A guest at a restaurant recently said to a Salvation

---

[2] W. E. Sangster, *The Secret of Radiant Life* (London: Hodder and Stoughton, 2nd Edition, 1963), 11.

2

Army friend of mine at the end of the meal, "I want what you've got." Many ways of sharing our faith have been developed in the past century. I believe that the vital issue of the *character* of the person sharing is all too often taken for granted. Christians are living and working alongside the unchurched every day, and when our character is radiant they will notice, and some will seek it. I think that is what God intended.

Two important factors are integrity and character. Billy Graham said,

> Integrity is the glue that holds our way of life together. We must constantly strive to keep our integrity intact. When wealth is lost, nothing is lost; when health is lost, something is lost; when character is lost, all is lost.[3]

Jesus declared that He is the Way, the Truth, and the Life (John 14:6). I have used that trilogy, as you will see, to group the different aspects of the message. Parts of this book will call for careful thought and I make no apologies for that. It will be worth it. If we are to discover and become all God wants us to be, there may be some unlearning of ideas we have picked up from our culture, but which contradict the teaching of the Bible. And our thinking must always be under the authority of scripture. I usually use the New King James Version for quotes, but occasionally the New Living Translation (NLT).

A word of deep appreciation is due to my wife Delcie for her encouragement as we have journeyed together now over many years. She has been the 'backbone' in so much of my work, and this resource has only been made possible because of her faithful behind-the-scenes assistance and attention to detail. I am also greatly indebted to the team of quality men and women who served as proof readers, for their invaluable editorial work. The congregations we have served have taught me so much, and I am deeply grateful for the privilege of the ministry. Dr Lindsay Cameron has been a friend over many years, and his encouragement has also been important to me.

The books listed in the Bibliography are ones I have referred to. In the Footnotes, I have used the term 'Ibid', which means that the quote referred to, comes from the source mentioned immediately

---

[3] Newsweek Magazine, 24 August 1987, 11. Quoted by John C. Maxwell, *Developing the Leader Within You* (Nashville: Thomas Nelson Publishers, 1993), 45.

before. With quotes from earlier writers I have, occasionally, modernized the language. Emphases in quotes are those of the original authors unless I have indicated otherwise.

The discussion questions in Appendix D are for your personal reflection after reading a chapter. The suggestions for their inclusion came from two close friends who indicated on scanning the material that they would like to use them for a small group series of studies, and so they have been prepared with that in view as well.

As you read, ask God to energize your mind as you think, and pray your way through the material. I trust these insights will stir you to greater heights in devotion and effective service for the Lord. May God expand your life until your destiny is fulfilled.

Sincerely

Don Hardgrave

PART 1: **THE LIFE**

The Life God Meant Us to Enjoy

Chapter 1

In many committed Christians, there is a longing for something better and there is no doubt about the possibility of a radiant character, as the Holy Spirit works increasingly in our lives. The content of our beliefs is important because this will affect our behaviour. Many are concerned about the Christianity of today, but the starting place for rebuilding must be with the kind of people who make up the church. We pray for revival, but what would it mean for each of us and our local churches? There is included an encouraging account of revival amongst the aboriginal people in Western Australia.

Chapter 2

We begin with a look at the disciples, clarifying God's working in their lives, in particular, those final days before Pentecost. This includes noting that there was a time-period between the Resurrection and that unforgettable time of their filling. After a close look at Jacob's life as an illustration of a pattern, there is a rare quote from one of the monks at the Dead Sea monastery on godliness. Then the lives of great saints are touched on, giving insight into their journey.

Chapter 3

There are testimonies of high moments in the lives of some famous men and women who have experienced a touch from God in recent centuries. Their backgrounds are so varied, but they all went on to greatness. Names include John Wesley, George Whitefield, Hudson Taylor, William and Catherine Booth, Samuel L. Brengle, Frances Ridley Havergal, Andrew Murray, Amy Carmichael, Watchman Nee, and some Australian ones. It was a fun chapter to prepare (apart from the tough decisions as to which ones to leave out—as there are so many available).

Chapter 4

The heart of the problem in the search for radiance is our inner civil war. We will look at suggested ways for people wanting to overcome their self-centredness, even as believers, and note relevant scriptures. The grand truth is that God *has* made provision for us to have a radiant character, and we need to learn how to access His resources. There is a helpful comparison of conversion with this new life of obedience (consecration).

Chapter 5

What is repentance and why does it matter? The word is seldom used today but the idea is really important for us to understand. Both John the Baptist and Jesus spoke of it at significant moments, as did the apostles. Also, the book of Revelation includes a similar call to churches. It is not just being sorry for the unhappy consequences of sin, rather we must learn to move on in harmony with the Holy Spirit. We consider the relevance of the call to repentance for us as Christians, with a powerful modern example, and application to today.

Chapter 1

The Need for a Radiant Character

Our longing for something better

I can still picture this lovely young woman in her late teens—we will call her Beth—singing passionately and obviously very sincerely in the worship team, "Every day, it's You I live for, every day, I will follow after You, every day, I will walk with You, my Lord." I can also picture her sometime later, when she came to my office for counselling, looking gaunt and thin earnestly asking me how to sustain her Christian life. I remember wondering afterwards whether she may have been on drugs at the time. Later, sadly, I was told that this was so and that she had encouraged others to use them as well.

So, how do we stop that kind of tragic slide away from a sincere walk with God? The question is not just for others; it also fits our *own* situation. How do we maintain the commitments we make to God at the start of our Christian journey right through to the end? Frankly, when I speak with God's people, many are honestly disappointed that their Christian life is missing something, but they are not sure what it is.

Why becoming radiant matters

Scripture repeatedly commands holiness for God's people. Consider Leviticus 11:44–45, 19:2 and 20:7 which is echoed in 1 Peter 1:15–16 as just one example: "... as He Who called you *is* holy, you also be holy in all your *conduct*, because it is written, '*Be holy, for I am holy.*'" The word 'holy' occurs ninety times in Leviticus and the Hebrew root word 152 times. Obviously, it is important to God.

Our craving for life's meaning will never be satisfied by anything less than applying God's will and His way in our daily lives. The truth is, we will never find the meaning and purpose we so desperately seek apart from earnestly seeking a closer relationship with God. Our developing holiness needs to be grounded in recognising Him as being both holy and righteous. Isaiah 6 affirms it similarly in the vision given to the prophet.

Spurgeon reaffirmed this experience of a radiant character as important for every believer. He spoke at the time when England and the British Empire were emerging as a super-power but with massive internal social issues. His impact upon his day and subsequent generations was profound. Consider the following:

> My brethren, there is a point in grace as much above the ordinary Christian, as the ordinary Christian is above the worldling. Believe me, the life of grace is no dead level, it is not a low country, a vast flat. There are mountains, and there are valleys. There are tribes of Christians who live in the valleys ... Such dwellers in the lowlands of unbelief, are for ever doubting, fearing, troubled about their interest in Christ, and tossed 'to and fro'; but there are other believers, who, by God's grace, have climbed the mountain of full assurance and close communion. Their place is with the eagle in his eyrie, high aloft.[1]

Clearly a spiritual awakening was needed then, just as it is needed today, and the message of which he spoke, is an essential part of that. Christmas Evans, the Welsh preacher, used by God in revivals, spoke of "God bending down to the dying embers of a fire just about to go out and breathing into it until it bursts into flame."[2]

The saintly Dr Sangster, writing from the bomb shelters of London during WW II, affirms the same truth:

> This is sure. There is an experience of God the Holy Spirit, available for all who will seek it with importunity, which imparts spiritual power far above the level enjoyed by the average Christian: which inspires a caring God-like love different in kind and degree from the affections of normal nature: which communicates to the eager soul the penetrating power of holiness. No book can give this experience. It belongs to the secret intercourse of the soul with God. It lies at the

---

[1] Charles H. Spurgeon, Quote from sermon No 880, 11/7/1869, *The Former and the Latter Rain*.
[2] Stuart Piggin, *Firestorm of the Lord* (Cumbria, UK: Paternoster Press, 2000), 19.

very heart of personal religion. Its wide reception would transform the Church and shake the world.[3]

He could write it because he had found it to be true. Alan Redpath comments:

The urgent need in the Church of Jesus Christ today is to learn how to deal with the tragic discrepancy between our profession and our experience.... I believe that the great trouble in the church today is a half-and-half salvation with which so many people seem to be perfectly satisfied. It is illustrated by Israel in the wilderness, between Egypt and Canaan, defeated and in bondage.[4]

Many years ago, I read a quote from E. M. Bounds which has stayed with me, "We do not need better methods or machinery, but better men [and women]." The power of the church to change society has always been through holy people, who radiated God's love. Consider Matthew 5:16: "Let your light so shine before men, that they may see your good works and glorify your Father in heaven."

Beliefs shape behaviour

It is obvious that what we value and believe influences what we do. This gives us a clue as to where to look for the key to the lock. For example, if you believe that the beggar on the street in Calcutta is being punished for wrong doing in a previous life (kind of like a jail sentence), then that will affect whether you put yourself out to help alleviate their suffering.

> What we value and believe influences what we do.

On the other hand, if you believe that the sufferer is precious to God, it will affect your way of relating to that person. It should not surprise us that the abolition of crucifixion, and later slavery, was initiated by the Christian church with its high view of God, and of people as having been made in His image. Consider the imbalance

---

[3] W. E. Sangster, *The Path to Perfection* (London: Hodder and Stoughton,1943), 7.
[4] Alan Redpath, *Victorious Christian Living—Studies in the Book of Joshua* (Basingstoke, Hants, UK: Pickering & Inglis, 1st British edition, 1956), 248–249.

between the numerous relief agencies founded by Christians and the comparative absence of such from our atheistic critics.

Are we 'on track' to become radiant personalities?

Biblical knowledge is at an all-time low. Today it is rare for unchurched parents to send their children to Sunday School, and often they will not even give permission for them to attend Religious Instruction at school. Many do not know what a Bible is, let alone what it contains. Sadly, many Christian parents do not make time in our busy society to teach their children at home either.

I am reminded of the counsel by Robert Coleman:

> In appraising the tragic condition of affairs today, we must not become frantic in trying to reverse the trend overnight. Perhaps that has been our problem. In our concern to stem the tide, we have launched one crash program after another to reach the multitudes with the saving Word of God.[5]

He then goes on to show that making disciples was the plan which Jesus used so successfully, and reminds us that leadership is a key.

Billy Graham also affirmed this importance. Consider the following:

> "Daddy, how can I believe in the Holy Spirit when I have never seen Him?" asked Jim. "I'll show you how," said his father, who was an electrician. Later Jim went with his father to the power plant where he was shown the generators. "This is where the power comes from to heat our stove and to give us light. We cannot see the power, but it is in that machine and in the power lines," said the father.
>
> "I believe in electricity," said Jim. "Of course, you do," said his father, "but you don't believe in it because you see it. You believe in it because you see what it can do. Likewise, you can believe in the Holy Spirit because you see what He does in people's lives when they are surrendered to Christ and possess His power."[6]

---

[5] Robert E. Coleman, *The Master Plan of Evangelism* (Old Tappan, NJ: Fleming H. Revell Company, 2nd Edition, 1964), 36.
[6] Billy Graham, *World Aflame* (Melbourne: William Heinemann Ltd., Australian Paperback edition, 1967), 156–157.

Graham then goes on to give a moving story of an alcoholic who had been converted at a crusade in London:

> The man phoned his psychiatrist [who had given up on him] and said: 'You have lost a patient. Christ has saved me from drink. I am now a new man.' The psychiatrist said, 'That sounds fine. Maybe I can find help where you found it. I am not an alcoholic, but I have my own needs and problems.' The psychiatrist began, too, to attend the meetings, and he, too, accepted Christ as his Saviour.[7]

> You can believe in the Holy Spirit because you see what He does in people's lives.
>
> - Billy Graham -

In Australia, we have had significant moves of the Holy Spirit as reflected in this exciting account by Arthur Malcolm, a Church Army evangelist and, from 1985, first Anglican Aboriginal Bishop about the coming of revival to Warburton and Meekatharra in 1981.

> God called all the Christians, and so-called Christians, together in a place called Cement Creek. There God called them to true repentance in heart and soul. The number of people there was 120. It's funny that that was the same number as in the book of Acts. We wonder was God saying something with a sense of humour; anyway God began to work ... doing wonders and miracles, and then the rain poured down to fill Cement Creek with water and the whole 120 were baptised. It didn't rain anywhere else—just where God began this work among the people.... An arrow in the sky told them to go and preach in the town of Warburton. 3,000 people came to the Lord and then 5,000 as they went on towards Meekatharra.... God used people with an open heart, people who were broken down but open to God. [8]

---

[7] Ibid., 160–161.
[8] Reported by Stuart Piggin, *Firestorm of the Lord*, 101–102.

Where to from here?

We may rightly ask what will be the fate of the once 'Christianised' West without revival. I believe it is for such a time as this that God has renewed the 'call to holiness'. The torch has been passed on to us. We can pray that God will set us aflame to light our world in its darkness.

This is not just an issue for the masses; it is the greatest need of each individual person. Unless you are totally available to God, He cannot use you greatly. You may choose 'to get by' but if you want a significant life that will really make a difference, you must be called out from the crowds, from mediocre Christianity, even from popularity, and let Jesus and His kingdom become your passion.

Stuart Piggin, an outstanding Australian author on revivals, declares:

If the Lord sent a revival to your church, what would happen? You would experience five things:

- A greatly enhanced sense of God's presence....
- A heightened responsiveness to God's word....
- An increased sensitivity to sin....
- An unprecedented sense of personal liberation....
- Unparalleled fruitfulness in your testimony for Christ....[9]

My own understanding of the message is perhaps best pictured by an incident as I was gardening. One of our boys brought me a drink of water with a huge smile on his toddler face. The plastic cup was not 100 percent spotless and the water was a bit above room temperature, but the 'moment' was his delight in doing something for his dad. As I drank, I found myself wondering if the Lord sees some of our stumbling efforts in His service and responds with like appreciation. So let's move to Chapter 2, clarifying the essential nature of the Christian faith and build from there.

---

[9] Ibid., 19–20.

Chapter 2

What Does It Mean to Be a Follower of Christ?

We do well to remember that the New Testament was written to people with a love for God, usually Christians, who were urged to move forward in relationship with Christ and to be filled with the Holy Spirit (Ephesians 5:18) as an ongoing experience. Thus, for those of us who love God and want to serve him more effectively, these encouragements are relevant for us as well.

Developing a relationship with Christ

Matthew concludes his gospel with the final words of Jesus:

Go therefore and make disciples of all the nations, baptizing them in the name of the Father, and of the Son and of the Holy Spirit, teaching them to observe all things that I have commanded you; and lo, I am with you always, even to the end of the age.[1]

Clearly Jesus wanted us to be like Him, and to help others become like Him as well. Hence it will be beneficial to consider the disciples' journey as a useful starting place.

The gospels tell us of the growth of the disciples' faith as sincere Jews, from an initial call to follow and become 'fishers of men' (Luke 5:10) until they heard, and no doubt, agreed with Peter's bold claim, "You are the Christ, the Son of the living God" (Matthew 16:16). They grew in their understanding of His role as Messiah—to die for the sins of the world and rise again on the third day. They finally 'got it' on Easter Sunday when He appeared and explained it all, from the post-resurrection perspective (Luke 24:44–46). No doubt Jesus went into much more depth with them over the next forty days, and His ascension made it clear that He would no longer be appearing and disappearing, as He had been doing.

---

[1] Matthew 28:19–20.

For several years, our family lived on an acreage in a small cottage. The colour scheme was canary yellow with blue trims. It was 'sad'. I repainted it a crisp white with lettuce green trims—much better. The only problem was that the spiders took advantage of the soft light on the eaves at night to build their webs there, so I was all too often cleaning them off. One day I said to my wife, "It's not enough to clean off webs, I'm going after the *spiders*." The transformation we are encouraged to seek through a relationship with Christ is a bit the same. We do not just want to get rid of this or that bad habit; we want to be changed on the inside into the image of Christ. Our selfishness is like the spider and it produces the 'webs' of sins. Coming to understand the difference is part of the preparation to be Spirit-filled.

Being filled with the Holy Spirit

For the next ten days after Jesus' ascension, the disciples stayed in Jerusalem, praying, growing spiritually (Acts 1:14), making decisions and, very likely, being reconciled where there were offences between them. By Pentecost, they had come to oneness (Acts 2:1), and suddenly they were all filled with the Holy Spirit (Acts 2:4). This does not mean the period between conversion and filling with the Holy Spirit for today's Christians must always be a set time or number of days, but it *does* suggest that there is usually a time between one and the other. The important thing is the certainty that a deeper work in the lives of believers as a result of the indwelling of the Holy Spirit is clearly taught in scripture. It is also evidenced in the lives of many outstanding Christian leaders whose fruit shows the divine endorsement of their ministry. The following chapters offer some answers to the questions this raises.

A good example of being transformed is seen in the life of Jacob, which has much to teach us. His character beforehand,[2] and his initial experience at Bethel have many parallels with conversion. The passage Genesis 28:1–22 shows that Jacob was willing to accept the Lord as his God on condition that:

He will be with him;
He will keep him safe;
He will provide food and clothing; and
He will bring him safely back home.

---

[2] Genesis 25:29–34, 27:1–29, 41–46.

To show he was genuine, Jacob set up a memorial pillar and promised the Lord a tithe. It was a beginning for him. God in his unbelievable mercy and grace 'took him on' and started the process of enabling him to become holy in this life. His name means 'trickster'. What a comfort we find in Psalm 46:11 that God calls himself the God of Jacob. There is hope for us yet! At the end of twenty years of 'wheeling and dealing' with Uncle Laban, Jacob was back again in his homeland, after fleeing from his uncle, but facing the prospect of meeting his brother Esau whom he had cheated so many years before. For him, this was a real crisis. If we review Genesis 28:18–22 where Jacob is setting conditions on his relationship with God; and compare it with Genesis 32 at Peniel, Jacob is a different man and the arrogance he showed earlier at Bethel is replaced by great fear and distress. He is

Claiming God's promises;
Acknowledging his unworthiness;
Expressing gratitude for God's goodness; and
Earnestly pleading for help.

Jacob's wrestling with the Stranger lasts all night and is a picture of the struggle so many Christians have before making a total commitment of their lives to God. At dawn, he receives a blessing from the Lord.

The other thing that is clear from Jacob's story is that it combines two different aspects with which we can readily identify:

- *Crisis*—moments when circumstances confront us with our need of God's help, and

- *Process*—the day-by-day results of seeking to live a life that is consistent with our previous commitments.

Clearly, this first decision to have the Lord as 'his God' does not exclude later times of consecration and re-commitment (Genesis 35:1–15).

Testimonies through the ages

The Old and New Testaments have other examples such as Moses' meetings with the Lord, which made his face shine (radiantly), and Isaiah's unforgettable vision where he 'saw the Lord'. Other prophets had visions which marked them out also. The New Testament letters and book of Acts record repeated actions of the Holy Spirit, to which we will refer.

The authors of the Dead Sea Scrolls came from a Jewish monastery prior to AD 70, and have become famous since the 1950s when translations began to become available to modern readers. The monks believed that,

> God will purge all the acts of man in the crucible of His truth … destroying every spirit of perversity from within his flesh and cleansing him by the Holy Spirit … that being made blameless in their ways, they may be endowed with inner vision.[3]

One of their hymns says,

> I know that no man can be righteous without your help. Wherefore I entreat you, through the Spirit which you have put within me, to bring unto completion the mercies you have shown your servant, cleansing him with your Holy Spirit … granting to him that place of favour which you have chosen for them that love you and observe your commandments, that they may stand in your presence forever.[4]

Lack of space limits treatment of the Middle Ages but, sadly, the church, after the late first century writer Clement, tended to link the search for holiness with the monasteries, with few exceptions. One of the dangers of a focus on a ritual or sacrament is that it is too easy to delude ourselves that we have done all that God requires. Consider the Old Testament prophets' call for *relationship with God* not mere externals (Micah 6:8). The same could apply to some churches of today. The period around the time of the Reformation saw a re-emergence of the quest for godliness outside of the monasteries, which has much to teach us. Here are a few samples from the 15th and 16th centuries and, in the next chapter, more recently.[5]

---

[3] IQS quoted by T. H. Gaster, *The Dead Sea Scriptures* (Doubleday, 1956), 45–46. This comes from George Allen Turner, *The Vision Which Transforms* (Kansas City, MO: Beacon Hill Press, 1964), 59.

[4] Ibid., 60.

[5] This has been an area where I have greatly enjoyed reading and learning of God's dealing with earnest believers in different ways but always for their growth. I especially recommend these three: George Turner, *The Vision Which Transforms*, V. Raymond Edman, *They Found the Secret* and James Gilchrist Lawson, *Deeper Experiences of Famous Christians*.

Girolamo Savonarola was an Italian monk whose ministry had a great effect on Florence and far beyond. He had unforgettable ministry moments including his personally approaching King Charles of France when the invading French army threatened Florence, and successfully persuading him to spare the town. His fiery preaching led the local citizens to build a huge pyramid of their masks, wigs, worldly books, obscene pictures, and the like. It was built in seven stages and was about twenty metres high and almost seventy-five metres around the base. It was burned amid the singing of hymns and the pealing of bells. He paid a price for his courageous confronting of evil, and was burned at the stake in 1498 at the express order of Pope Alexander VI, but was not forgotten by the people for his faithfulness to God. However, the key moments were earlier when Savonarola deepened his commitment and one day felt a vision and call to serve by calling the people back to God.[6]

> Savonarola deepened his commitment and one day felt a vision and call to serve by calling the people back to God.

George Fox also had special visions and a strong burden to turn people's eyes from the outward forms to the real priorities of a holy heart and life. Although the theology and ceremonials of Fox and Savonarola differed widely in view of their denominational settings, the emphases of Christ-likeness and heart purity were wonderfully evident. A contemporary of Jeremy Taylor, Fox refused to limit holiness to the monastery and saw it as a vital basis for social concern and activism.[7]

Madam Guyon lived in France in the reign of Louis XIV and her childhood was marked by poor health and an unhappy marriage at 16. It was when she was 20 that a conversation with a relative who had served as a missionary to China stirred her to seek God more earnestly. On the basis of faith and the lessons learned in the ups and

---

[6] James Gilchrist Lawson, *Deeper Experiences of Famous Christians* (Anderson, IN: The Warner Press, 1911), 63–67.
[7] Keith Drury, (David W. Holdren, Editor), *Holiness for Ordinary People* (Marion, IN: The Wesley Press, 1983), 33.

downs of her previous searching, she developed a more settled and deep love for God. She said to a Franciscan monk who earlier had been a tremendous help to her in spiritual things:

> I love God far more than the most affectionate lover among men loves the object of his earthly attachment. This love of God occupied my heart so constantly and strongly, that it was very difficult for me to think of anything else. Nothing else seemed worth attention.[8]

In the years that followed she wavered between lapses and times of growth including when she read the works of Thomas á Kempis and shared with other devoted believers. Tragedies and times of depression, drove her closer to God. On July 22, 1680, aged 32, she had a deepening of the earlier closeness of God and enjoyed a deeper awareness of God. She was able to influence the outstanding Archbishop Fenelon and her writings were very widely read throughout France. Many were written when she was imprisoned for her faith in various parts of the country, and Guyon's influence has extended around the world.

Archbishop Fenelon was also called to serve in the days of Louis XIV, and he was mistreated for his emphasis on the holy life. The term he used was the 'crucified life', linked with Galatians 2:20. He found great encouragement in his times face to face with Madam Guyon and in extended correspondence with her. On many occasions, she testified to considerable time spent praying for him— sometimes all night. The heart of the struggle was abandoning himself fully to the will of God, but that day did come. He was opposed by the king and effectively exiled to a small parish, as well as being severely criticised by a determined opponent, Bishop Bousset. Fenelon set out his understanding of the holy life in six steps—summarized below:

- Bring all natural appetites under God's control.

- Cease to focus on inward feelings of relief which came with an initial conversion experience.

- Take primary satisfaction not from any inward virtues but rather from the Giver of all gifts.

- Accept all the sufferings and blows of life's journey with cheerfulness.

---

[8] Lawson, *Deeper Experiences of Famous Christians*, 75.

- Cease to take joy in outward things that we might find our joy in Him—letting God live and act in every area of our lives.

- Ensure that there is complete harmony between our will and His, as Paul put it, "It is no longer I who live but Christ lives in me."[9]

Fenelon's writings had a great influence across France extending beyond mere devotional works. One possible cause of the fanatical opposition from Louis, was Fenelon's ideas on needed political change in France. Perhaps if he had been heeded, the tragedy of future political terror may have been avoided or at least lessened.

John Bunyan was born of humble circumstances around the same time in England. He was to greatly influence the world by his writing of an allegory *Pilgrim's Progress*. Bunyan was a tinker (repairer of pots and pans) and later joined the army. He came close to death by drowning, an encounter with a poisonous snake, and also in the military. He describes himself as *"swearing, cursing and blaspheming the name of God"*. So much was this so, that a lady feared lest he *"corrupt the whole youth of the town"*.[10] This rebuke caused him to cut off swearing and begin to read the Bible, but he had not yet found peace and joy.

Bunyon was influenced by a talk with three women who were sitting speaking about the things of God, and then by his pastor Mr. Gifford who was, no doubt, the Evangelist in *Pilgrim's Progress*. Many of the chapters of the book reflect his own journey, including the 'Slough of Despond', reaching the foot of the cross where his burden fell away, and the castle of 'Giant Despair'—where the key of promise opened every door in 'Doubting Castle'. My favourite chapter is the house of the interpreter where he sits with 'the best of books in his hand and his gaze up to heaven'.

He wrote of a day, when he was passing through a field and the thoughts came to him that his 'righteousness is in heaven'. These were so powerful that with the eye of faith he saw Jesus at God's right hand and declared "Now did my chains fall off my legs indeed; I was loosed from my afflictions and irons; ...." He concluded, "now went I also home rejoicing, for the grace and love of God."[11]

---

[9] Ibid., 86–88.
[10] Ibid., 111.
[11] Ibid., 113.

This did not mean that the journey was an easy one, and Bunyan was imprisoned for 12 years for holding meetings separate from the Church of England, but his influence has been widespread. This applies especially to his emphases on grace, assurance, having no fear of death, and fruitful service.

There are more testimonies as examples in the next chapter, but the following overview will serve as a bridge to them.

The big picture

Regarding any deeper work of the Holy Spirit, we must consider three misconceptions.

1) My experience has to be the same as someone else's or it is not the real thing (See Chapter 3).

2) Holiness makes you faultless (See Chapter 6).

3) Holiness sets you above temptation (See Chapter 7).

Defining our terms

Paul's letter to the Romans deals very systematically with this whole issue and reaches a wonderful climax in Chapter 5:1 that "having been justified by faith, we have peace with God through our Lord Jesus Christ." He then addresses the ongoing struggle with what is, in older translations, called 'the old man'. Before sharing the victory of Chapter 8, he graphically describes himself as a 'wretched man' needing delivery from this 'body of death'. Hence, there follows the message of triumph through 'the power of the life-giving Spirit which sets us free from the law of sin and death' (7:28–8:2). It is this issue which is the central topic of the book you are reading.

The invention of the printing press made wide distribution of the Bible available as never before, and so there has been a steady stream of Christians discovering this wonderful truth, but their different settings meant that the ways of describing it have differed. With this in view you will find Appendix A has a page of definitions. It is worth your taking a moment to review these. I will be using several important terms and the stream which I have found most helpful flows from the 18th century Methodists. I will use that framework, but not to exclude other authors. I have found Reformed writers like Jerry Bridges and Martyn Lloyd-Jones extremely helpful and I trust that readers familiar with different usage will keep reading!

We have recognised that God is holy and wants his people to be holy, and that this holds the key to new hope for our world through a revival, or spiritual awakening.

Wesleyan historian, Roy S. Nicholson, gives this helpful summary:

[The Christian] is holy in the sense that he is morally pure. He is sinless in the sense that his past sinful acts have all been pardoned and his corrupt nature cleansed. He is blameless in the sense that God sees in his pardoned and cleansed soul nothing condemned by the Gospel law. As to his love it is perfect in kind, and perfect in the sense that he loves with all the heart, mind, soul, and strength; and in the sense, that "love is the fulfilling of the law".... His soul ... now matures in degree, and ripens for glorification.[12]

In Chapter 7 you will find further comments on the term 'perfect' as it is used in scripture.

> God is holy and wants his people to be holy, and this holds the key to new hope for our world through a revival, or spiritual awakening.

An important clarification

The command to be filled with the Holy Spirit has been understood in different ways today, in that many believe that the sign of this wonderful work is the experience of 'speaking in an unknown tongue'. There is a special and very helpful chart on this at the end of Appendix A.

---

[12] Kenneth Geiger (Compiler), *Insights into Holiness:* Chapter by Roy S. Nicholson, *Holiness and the Human Element* (Kansas City, MO: Beacon Hill Press, 1963), 170–171.

Chapter 3

Testimonies—More Than 'Fire Insurance'

The continuing work of the Holy Spirit

If we consider a magnet (lodestone), it looks similar to other pieces of steel but careful observation reveals that there is an unseen power at work. It is attracted to some pieces of steel, unaffected by others such as stainless steel, and even repelled by the opposite end of another magnetized piece. Similarly, believers filled with the Holy Spirit will be welcomed by some, ignored by some, and with yet others be repelled and even persecuted.

The long history of the Christian church has many accounts of outstanding people who were touched by God and never the same afterward, making an impact on their world out of all proportion to their numbers. They are the proof that the holy life holds a key to meeting the challenge of every age, with grace, holy love, and courage. This chapter is devoted to a brief overview of some, whose lives became widely known in the modern era.

As believers, there usually came a moment of crisis or full commitment which was preceded and followed by growth in godliness and love for God, plus the passion for the truths of scripture. However, the reader will note that each person had a varied journey as God loves to treat us all as uniquely different.

John Wesley (UK): The life of Wesley adds significantly to this study, not just in his own story, but also because his teaching held together both truth and experience. He expressed this message in his writings, preaching, and songs.[1] He was born at a strategic time in world history around the time of the industrial revolution and ministered in that unsettled period as many in the rural sector

---

[1] John Wesley translated many hymns from German, and his brother Charles wrote over 8,000 hymns, many of which are outstanding, and still used today.

moved to the cities. He was remarkably successful[2] and we can learn from him as we live in a 'computer chip' revolution. (For the purpose of this book, I am thinking mainly of his small group model to which we will refer in Chapter 11.) There is also his scriptural teaching on holiness.

His parents had a Puritan upbringing, (before they returned to the Anglican church) and his education was thorough, both at home, and in the public contexts later. He was outstanding at Oxford, gaining an MA and was given the status of 'Fellow' of Lincoln college. His journey to find the deeper life, became focused when he (aged 22) read the mystics including Thomas á Kempis, *The Imitation of Christ,* and later William Law, *Serious call to a Devout and Holy Life and* Jeremy Taylor, *Holy Living and Dying.*

While at Oxford he became leader of a small group (called in derision, the 'Holy Club', the 'Bible Moths', or the 'Methodists') who visited prisons, helped the sick and contributed to the education of children as they sought to apply the things they learned from their times together studying scripture. In 1735, he and his brother Charles sailed for America. He wanted to evangelise the Indians, but after two unfruitful years, he returned very discouraged and humbled. His experiences on the trips included an incident in a severe storm when the vessel seemed doomed, and he noticed that the German missionaries were unafraid of death—singing songs when all the others were terrified. Conversations with some of their leaders helped clarify his need to have a faith that went beyond mere assent to theological statements. His dying father stressed 'the inner witness' (1 John 5:10) or 'assurance', and this was his search.

The moment came at a small meeting in 1738, when one was reading Luther's preface to Paul's letter to the Romans and explaining the place of faith. His heart was 'strangely warmed' and all the discipline he had learned in earlier years, especially in mysticism, now served his mission to *'reform the nation, particularly the church and spread scriptural holiness across the land.'*[3] Reputable historians affirm that he and his preacher friends saved England from a tragic

---

[2] His use of circuits to share preachers among several congregations, is a brilliant idea (and biblical—consider Samuel and Paul as examples) which others, including the author, have used successfully in planting churches.

[3] This resolution was passed at the first Methodist Conference in 1744 as their 'mission statement'.

Revolution such as overtook France in 1789.[4] Here is his famous quote about his message:

> This doctrine [entire sanctification] is *the grand depositum* which God has lodged with the people called Methodists; and for the sake of propagating this chiefly He appeared to have raised us up.[5]

One historian writes, "The passionate evangelism of the early Methodists ... would simply have gone for nothing if the holy lives of the early Methodists had not backed up the evangelistic appeal."[6] Do not underestimate the impact of the 'Awakening' on the nation which flowed through other denominations such as the Anglicans encouraging their evangelical wing, and Daniel Taylor greatly expanding the Baptists.

A detail sadly missed by some today is Wesley's stress on the need for ongoing diligence. He stressed that there is no height of holiness from which it is impossible to fall in this life. When Wesley spoke of holiness, he preferred to use the words 'Christian perfection' and defined it as a 'perfection of love for God and my neighbour'.[7]

George Whitefield (UK and USA): Space does not permit detailed treatment of Wesley's close friend whose experience of a deeper work came at his ordination to the ministry. He became a member of the Holy Club and had an outstanding gift of preaching. Whitfield began open-air ministry to the miners in Bristol and when he went to America he encouraged Wesley to pick up and continue this. Later, he and Wesley differed on the subject of election (emphasising God's predestining work in the life of the believer) but they were one on the emphasis of a holy life and the importance of making a full commitment to God.[8]

John Fletcher (UK): The other Methodist of the period who deserves special mention was Swiss born, came to England to learn

---

[4] This original is traced to French historian, Elie Halevy, See
  https://www.jstor.org/stable/3165098
[5] J. Wesley: *Letters 8:238.* Quoted in A. Skevington Wood, *The Burning Heart* (London: The Paternoster Press, 1967), 260.
[6] Wood, *The Burning Heart*, 262.
[7] Steve DeNeff, *More Than Forgiveness* (Indianapolis, IN: Wesleyan Publishing House, 2002), 90.
[8] Lawson, *Deeper Experiences of Famous Christians*, 131–136.

the language, and while there had a vivid dream concerning the final judgement such that he began to search for peace with God. He heard that the Methodists "did nothing but pray" so he found them and was greatly helped. Here is his testimony: "All my righteousness is as filthy rags. I am a very devil, though of an inferior sort, and if I am not renewed before I go hence, hell will be my portion for all eternity." This was followed by a period of earnest confession and one day several scriptures spoke especially to his need.... "Cast your burden on the Lord and he will sustain you. He will not suffer the righteous to be moved.... I will be with you; fear not, neither be dismayed.... Whatsoever you shall ask in My Name, I will do it."[9]

Lawson adds the following comment:

> Like Wesley, [Fletcher] believed that while men are imperfect in knowledge and in many other ways, it is possible for them to be perfect in love, or to love God with all the strength and intelligence they possess. He believed that the promise of the baptism of the Holy Spirit was for believers today as much as at the day of Pentecost.[10]

William and Catherine Booth (global ministry): Another couple with similar outstanding ministry were the Booths. William was born into an Anglican family but while still a youth changed and regularly worshipped at the Wesleyan chapel. At the age of 13 he made a commitment to Christ. Raised in extreme poverty he early developed a concern for the lower classes and was reinforced in that, by Wesley's example and teaching. He was fearful of public speaking, but after much prayer he tried speaking and reading some scriptures on a street corner where he was jeered at, and stones were thrown at him. (He later became a master at mass evangelism, and loved to speak of 'the blessing of a clean heart'.)

He gained an apprenticeship and soon after, was encouraged to become a minister. He married Catherine Mumford when his finances permitted, and they served the Lord together very effectively, moving into independent evangelism. After carefully studying Wesley's writings together, they sought the experience of sanctification and here are Catherine's words:

---

[9] Ibid., 139.
[10] Ibid., 140.

My soul has been much called out of late on the doctrine of holiness. I feel that hitherto we have not put it in a sufficiently definite and tangible manner before the people—I mean as a specific and attainable experience. Oh, that I had entered into the fulness of the enjoyment of it myself. I intend to struggle after it. In the mean time we have commenced already to bring it specifically before our dear people.[11]

In another letter speaking of sanctification, she says "William has preached on it twice, and there is a glorious quickening amongst the people."[12] The Booths continued to be very effective and in 1865, they began a work in the east end of London which was to become the Salvation Army in 1877. Gradually the unique characteristics were added, a military-like structure, the band, the uniform and the ladies' bonnet (designed by Catherine to protect their heads from rocks that were being thrown). In just over 25 years their work extended to over 55 different countries. Their mottos of 'Soap, Soup and Salvation' and 'Less Creed and More Deed' sum up the thrust of reaching the poor, but the heart of their message was not just salvation but the holy life.[13] Booth comments:

I consider that the chief dangers which confront the coming century will be religion without the Holy Spirit, Christianity without Christ; forgiveness without repentance; salvation without regeneration; politics without God; and Heaven without Hell.[14]

Dwight L Moody (global ministry) had received very little education but he made a huge impact for God in the UK and the USA. He witnessed to all he could contact, during the American Civil War, with apparent effectiveness in those early years, and yet in his own heart there was a deep dissatisfaction that increased to the point of desperation. One evening as he was entering the carriage to go on to another meeting, an old man said to him to "honour the Holy Spirit" and Moody testified that from that day on he remembered those words and the old finger pointing to him. Then, there were two godly women who prayed that he would be "filled with the Holy Spirit". After the great Chicago fire, the work Moody had founded was in

[11] Ibid., 255.
[12] Ibid., 255.
[13] Ibid., 251.
[14] www.christianquotes.info/quotes-by-author/william-booth-quotes/ #axzz4o5vBq0OI.

ruins and he went east to raise funds and there experienced a newness of the Spirit. Raymond Edman has quoted Moody's own words and added a summary:

> [Moody wrote] "My heart was not in the work of begging. I could not appeal. I was crying all the time that God would fill me with His Spirit. Well, one day, in the city of New York,—oh what a day!—I cannot describe it, I seldom refer to it; it is almost too sacred an experience to name. Paul had an experience of which he never spoke for fourteen years. I can only say that God revealed Himself to me, and I had such an experience of His love that I had to ask Him to stay His hand. I went to preaching again. The sermons were not different; I did not present any new truths, and yet hundreds were converted. I would not now be placed back where I was before that blessed experience if you should give me all the world—it would be as the small dust of the balance." [Edman concludes] The sermons were not different; but the servant was![15]

> The sermons were not different;
> but the servant was!
>
> - Edman -

The following are two quotes from a message he preached on his return from the UK:

> A thought I want to call your attention to is this, that God has got a good many children who have just barely got life, but no power for service. You might say safely ... that nineteen out of every twenty professed Christians are of no earthly account so far as building up Christ's kingdom; but on the contrary, they are standing right in the way, and the reason is because they have just got life and have settled down, and have not sought for power. The Holy Spirit coming upon them with power is distinct and separate from conversion. If the Scripture doesn't teach it I am ready to correct it.[16]

---

[15] V. Raymond Edman, *They Found the Secret* (London: Marshall, Morgan and Scott, 1st British Edition, 1961), 83–84.
[16] Ibid., 85.

He continues:

A great many think because they have been filled once, they are going to be full for all time after; but O, my friends, we are leaky vessels, and have to be kept right under the fountain all the time in order to keep full. If we are going to be used by God we have to be very humble. A man that lives close to God will be the humblest of men. I heard a man say that God always chooses the vessel that is close at hand. Let us keep near Him.[17]

Amy Carmichael (India): It was while helping a bedraggled elderly woman on a street in Belfast (Ireland) because she felt sorry for her, that her life's values were changed for ever. Feeling embarrassed that people would 'look down on her' for helping such a woman, it was as though she heard a voice saying to her that "all our work will one day be tested by fire and that only those things that had eternal value would survive." She thus determined from then on 'to hold her head high' and seek only to please God. Later that day, Amy (then 18 years old) shut herself in her room and settled finally the pattern of her future life. She had made a commitment to the Lord two years earlier but this was a *complete* one and led on to missionary service.

Initially, she began overseas service in Japan, but then moved to India where she remained for 55 years. During her time there she took every opportunity to share Christ with those she met. She was horrified to find out that young girls (even babies) were left at the Hindu temple to begin a life of prostitution. Her heart was filled with compassion and thus she began taking girls (and later boys) into her care. Over the years she provided for hundreds of unwanted children.

Well known for her writing ministry, Amy penned the following which perhaps, in fact, summed up her life's calling:

If you hold fast to the resolve that in all things Christ as Lord shall have the pre-eminence, if you keep His will, His glory, and His pleasure high above everything, and if you continue in His love, loving one another as He has loved you, then all will be well, eternally well.[18]

---

[17] Ibid., 86.
[18] Ibid., 41.

It is no wonder that Edman, entitled this chapter of his book: *Amy Carmichael: The Radiant Life.*

Charles G. Finney (USA) was raised in the backwoods in New York (state), and trained as a school teacher and a lawyer. He didn't understand Bible terms but accepted it as the Word of God. This led him to read it and he began to see the importance of the saving of his own soul. It was in this frame of mind that the following account comes from his own pen:

> On a Sabbath evening in the autumn of 1821, I made up my mind that I would settle the question of my soul's salvation at once, that if it were possible I would make my peace with God. But as I was very busy with the affairs of the office, I knew that without great firmness of purpose, I should never effectually attend to the subject.[19]

He describes how the next few days were a blend of strengthened convictions and a hardness of heart. He continues describing, in particular, his visit to the woods nearby, to be alone. On his knees, he affirmed commitment to God resulting in a string of comforting verses coming to his mind.[20] That evening, alone in his office, he had a vision of Jesus Who appeared to him and he unexpectedly received a filling with the Holy Spirit. Let him continue:

> ...the Holy Spirit descended upon me in a manner that seemed to go through me, body and soul. I could feel the impression, like a wave of electricity, going through and through me. Indeed, it seemed to come in waves and waves of liquid love; for I could not express it in any other way. It seemed like the very breath of God. I can recollect distinctly that it seemed to fan me, like immense wings.[21]

Samuel Logan Brengle (USA) was a Methodist called by God to become part of the Salvation Army and he exercised a remarkable ministry. Describing his change beyond conversion, he writes:

> I saw the humility of Jesus, and my pride; the meekness of Jesus, and my temper; the lowliness of Jesus, and my ambition; the purity of Jesus, and my unclean heart; the faithfulness of

---

[19] Ibid., 50.
[20] Edman correctly identifies this as his conversion. Ibid., 56.
[21] Ibid., 55. This material is obviously from Finney's writings as it is also word for word in Lawson, *Deeper Experiences of Famous Christians*, 175–185. Both books have extended, useful quotes longer than space permits in this book.

Jesus, and the deceitfulness of my heart; the unselfishness of Jesus, and my selfishness; the trust and faith of Jesus, and my doubts and unbelief; the holiness of Jesus, and my un-holiness. I got my eyes off everybody but Jesus and myself and I came to loathe myself....

> This is the perfect love about which the Apostle John wrote; but it is beyond all I dreamed of; in it is personality; this love thinks, wills, talks with me, corrects me, instructs and teaches me.
>
> - Brengle -
>
> [22]

I shall never forget my joy, mingled with awe and wonder, when this dawned upon my consciousness. For several weeks I had ... been crying to God almost day and night for a pure heart and the baptism with the Holy Spirit, when ... this text suddenly opened to my understanding: "If we confess our sins, He is faithful and just to forgive our sins, and to cleanse us from all unrighteousness"; and I was enabled to believe ... that the precious Blood cleansed my heart, even mine, from all sin.... my heart was melted like wax before fire; Jesus Christ was revealed to my spiritual consciousness, revealed in me, and my soul was filled with unutterable love. I walked in a heaven of love. Then one day, with amazement, I said to a friend: 'This is the perfect love about which the Apostle John wrote; but it is beyond all I dreamed of; in it is personality; this love thinks, wills, talks with me, corrects me, instructs and teaches me.' And then I knew that God the Holy Spirit was in this love and this love was God, for 'God is love'.... I have never doubted this experience since. I have sometimes wondered whether I might not have lost it.... In time, God withdrew something of the tremendous emotional feelings. He taught me I had to live by my faith and not by my emotions.... He showed me that I must learn to trust Him ... regardless of how I felt.[23]

---

[22] Samuel L Brengle, *When the Holy Ghost is Come* (New York: Cosimo Classics, 2005), 11.
[23] Edman, *They Found the Secret*, 24–27.

A few 'thumbnail sketches'

This material is so important, that I am reluctant to omit other writers, but the purpose of this book is to major on the 'How', especially the 'How to maintain' the blessing after God meets us. Hence, I will have to be content just to give snippets from other outstanding believers whom God has greatly used. It is well worthwhile researching the whole story of each of their lives.

Lionel Fletcher (Australia): Stuart Piggin in his excellent book on revival, *Firestorm of the Lord*, parallels the experience of Wesley, Finney, Moody and then writes about an Australian, Lionel Fletcher:

> ... possibly the most prominent evangelist Australia has ever produced, experienced in 1897, the year after his conversion, and about which he testified, 'My life was never the same again and every blessing I have received since, every soul won, and every Church revived in my ministry, is a result of that night."[24]

J. Hudson Taylor (founder of the China Inland Mission) was touched by reading a letter from his friend John McCarthy, who wrote:

> To let my loving Saviour work in me His will, my sanctification is what I would live for by His grace. Abiding, not striving nor struggling; looking off unto Him; trusting Him for present power; trusting Him to subdue all inward corruption; resting in the love of an almighty Saviour, in the conscious joy of a complete salvation, a salvation 'from all sin' ... willing that His will should truly be supreme this is not new, and yet 'tis new to me. I feel as though the first dawning of a glorious day had risen upon me.[25]

> [Taylor read McCarthy's letter] in the little mission station at Chia-kiang on Saturday, September 4, 1869... [He said:] "As I read, I saw it all. I looked to Jesus; and when I saw, oh how the joy flowed!"... Writing to his sister in England, he said: "As to work, mine was never so plentiful, so responsible, or so difficult; but the weight and strain are all gone."[26]

---

[24] Piggin, *Firestorm of the Lord*, 99.
[25] Edman, *They Found the Secret*, 18.
[26] Ibid., 19.

Frances Ridley Havergal (UK) came from a pastor's home and early learned the truth of the gospel but also that she must personally commit to its message. It seems that God sometimes uses a book or piece of literature, and a small book *All for Jesus* was instrumental in leading her to the crisis of faith. She read and re-read it and wrote in her journal, "I do so long for deeper and fuller teaching in my own heart. *All for Jesus* has touched me very much...."[27]

This is what she shared with her sister Maria later:

First, I was shown that 'the blood of Jesus Christ His Son cleanseth us from all sin' and then it was made plain to me that He who had thus cleansed me had power to keep me clean; so I just utterly yielded myself to Him, and utterly trusted Him to keep me.[28]

Frances' faith rose to the challenge of her poor health and when friends sympathised with her in her final illness, she declared, "Never mind! It's home the faster! God's will is *delicious*; He makes no mistakes."[29] Her songs include *Like a River Glorious is God's Perfect Peace, Lord Speak to Me,* as well as *Take My Life.*

> I just utterly yielded myself to Him,
> and utterly trusted Him to keep me.
>
> - Havergal -

John Watsford was the first Australian-born Methodist clergyman. He was praying with two friends three times every day for an outpouring of the Holy Spirit. He recounts what happened:

At the end of the fourth week, on Sunday evening, ... people flocked to the prayer-meeting, till the schoolroom was filled.... The minister ... was concluding with the benediction ... he stopped, and sobbed aloud. When he could speak he called out, 'Brother Watsford, pray.' I prayed, and then my two friends prayed, and oh! the power of God that came upon the people, who were overwhelmed by it in every part of the

---

[27] Edman, *They Found the Secret*, 73–74.
[28] Ibid, also in Lawson, *Deeper Experiences of Famous Christians*, 320.
[29] Lawson, *Deeper Experiences of Famous Christians*, 326.

room! And what a cry for mercy! It was heard by the passers-by in the street, some of whom came running in to see what was the matter, and were smitten down at the door in great distress.... Day after day and week after week the work went on, and many were converted. Among them many young persons.[30]

That was Parramatta in 1840 but he went on to have an effective ministry in NSW and the Darling Downs in Queensland (as well as in Fiji). The revivals were not exclusively Methodist, and between 1858 and 1860, the Manning River saw "one of the most remarkable awakenings of the Spirit of God that we know in Australia's history" under Rev. Allan McIntyre, a Presbyterian.[31]

John Hyde (India): A letter confronted the missionary en-route to India. It said he needed to be filled with the Holy Spirit. At first, he crumpled it up but later unfolded it and prayed claiming the promise 'you shall receive power after the Holy Spirit has come upon you.' The fruit of his ministry showed the difference it made but there were also times of earnest seeking after God over later years. His prayer life was an inspiration to many. On one occasion, he was reluctant to share some of his prayers but finally yielded after which there was a revival among the missionaries which spread to the populace.[32]

F.B. Meyer (UK) writes:

I had been a minister of a large influential church, but I was very unhappy, for I was conscious that I had not received the power of the Holy Spirit. Then I went to that little village, Keswick, where a great number of God's people had gathered to seek and receive the power of the Holy Spirit. One night they had elected to have a prayer meeting from nine o'clock to eleven and onwards to pray for the Holy Spirit. I joined them ... [but after a few hours I left] and I crept out into the lane away from the village. As I walked I said. "Oh my God, if there is a man in this village who needs the power of the Holy Spirit to rest upon him, it is I; but I do not know how to receive Him ..."

---

[30] Iain H. Murray, *Australian Christian Life From 1788* (Edinburgh: The Banner of Truth Trust, 1988), 153.

[31] Piggin, *Spirit of a Nation* (Sydney: Strand Publishing, 2004), 42–43. Piggin also gives examples in Victoria and South Australia.

[32] Edman, *They Found the Secret*, Chapter 10.

A voice said to me, "As you took forgiveness from the hand of the dying Christ, *take the Holy Spirit* from the hand of the living Christ." I turned to Christ and said, "Lord, as I breathe in this whiff of warm night air, so I breathe into every part of me Thy blessed Spirit." I felt no hand laid upon my head; there was no lambent flame; there was no rushing sound from heaven. *But by faith*, without emotion and without excitement, I took for the first time, *and I have kept on taking ever since....* I turned to leave the mountain side, and as I went down, the tempter said, ... "Do you feel it?" I said, "I do not." [The tempter replied], "Then if you do not feel it, you have not got it." I said, "I do not feel it, but I reckon that God is faithful ... I know I have Him because God led me to put in my claim."[33]

> I have learnt to place myself before God every day, as a vessel to be filled with His Holy Spirit.
>
> - Murray -

Andrew Murray (South Africa): For several years after his conversion, Murray felt there was something lacking in his life. Then one day a missionary said to him, "Brother, remember that when God puts a desire into your heart, He will fulfil it." For several years he kept on asking and seeking. Until one day he deepened his commitment and describes it as follows:

I gave myself to God as perfectly as I could to receive the baptism of the Spirit. Yet there was failure ... It was somehow as if I could not get what I wanted. Through all these stumblings God led me, without any special experience that I can point to, but as I look back I do believe now that He was giving me more and more of His Blessed Spirit, had I but known it better.... I have learnt to place myself before God every day, as a vessel to be filled with His Holy Spirit.[34]

---

[33] T. A. Hegre, *The Cross and Sanctification* (Minneapolis, MN: Bethany Fellowship, Inc., 1960), 138–140.
[34] Edman, *They Found the Secret*, 96.

Watchman Nee (China) was converted while a college student in 1920. About seven years after this came a discovery which marked a deeper work and a turning point in his journey:

> I was upstairs sitting at my desk reading the Word and praying, and I said, 'Lord, open my eyes!' And then in a flash I saw it. I saw my oneness with Christ. I saw that I was in Him, and that when He died I died. I saw that the question of my death was a matter of the past and not of the future, and that I was just as truly dead as He was because I was in Him when He died. The whole thing had dawned upon me. I was carried away with such joy at this great discovery that I jumped from my chair and cried, 'Praise the Lord, I am dead!' I ran downstairs and met one of the brothers helping in the kitchen and laid hold of him. 'Brother', I said, 'do you know that I have died?' I must admit he looked puzzled. 'What do you mean?' he said, so I went on: 'Do you not know that Christ has died? Do you not know that I died with Him? Do you not know that my death is no less truly a fact than His?' Oh it was so real to me! I longed to go through the streets of Shanghai shouting the news of my discovery. From that day to this I have never for one moment doubted the finality of that word: "I have been crucified with Christ".[35]

Kingsley Ridgway (Australia), had a long quest for salvation, and when it finally came he wrote:

> I was borne away out on the vast sea of God's eternal love, where there was no ripple, no bottom, no shore; and such a sense of calm, sweet, uncaring peace throbbed in my soul that death, nor life, nor angels, nor principalities nor powers nor height nor depth nor any other creature disturbed those blissful moments of ecstatic communion with my Maker .... my heart was singing within me, for the long, long night had gone, the Dayspring from on high had visited me. My burden was gone. I had the victory. My search was ended. I had found God![36]

---

[35] Watchman Nee, *The Normal Christian Life* (London: Victory Press, Revised Edition, 1963), 43-44.

[36] Kingsley M. Ridgway, *In Search of God—An Account of Ministerial Labours in Australia and the Islands of the Sea*, 1937. Republished in *Pioneer with a Passion*, 2nd edition, ed. Lindsay Cameron (Australia: Wesleyan Methodist Church, 2011), 182.

Sometime later, he was filled with the Holy Spirit and described it thus:

> The first time the power fell on me was at the first of these all night meetings. We were standing up singing, "There is power, power, wonder-working power, in the precious blood of the Lamb", when the heavens seemed to open, and a stream of glory poured upon my soul from the upper sanctuary. When I came to myself I was lying under the table, and the service was proceeding quite nicely without me. Many times since then those shocks of power have fallen on me, and I am free to confess they never come too often to be badly needed.[37]

Norman Vincent Peale (USA) was sharing his discouragement with his wife and she urged him to cry to the Lord in total surrender.

> "Dear Lord Jesus." he prayed, "I cannot handle my life. I need help. I need You. I hereby with all my heart surrender my mind, my soul, my life to You. Use me as You will. Fill me with Your Holy Spirit."... Then it happened; such peace as I would never have dreamed possible surged through me, and with it a burst of joy. It was like light, like glory.... I leaped to my feet and began to pace up and down. ... [He then said to his wife,] "let's go back home. Let's get to work. We're going to have the time of our life, all of our life![38]

George Henry Morling (Australia), principal of the Baptist Theological College in NSW, was passionate about the filling of the Holy Spirit. It was said of him that:

> [he] lived the doctrine of the Holy Spirit. That was his major teaching. Not the present razzmatazz, but the old time genuine understanding of the indwelling Spirit of Christ in a man's life and it was reflected through him.... In 1942 he confided in his diary that he longed to be filled with the Holy Spirit.... [He] longed for 'definite power above mere influence', for him truth had to be on fire, doctrine had to be experiential, and spirituality had to be efficient, by which he meant effective in the real world.[39]

---

[37] Ibid., 195.
[38] Norman Vincent Peale, *The Positive Power of Jesus Christ* (London: Hodder and Stoughton, 1981), 51–52.
[39] Stuart Piggin, *Spirit of a Nation* (Sydney: Strand Publishing, 2004), 100–101.

Billy Graham (global ministry) received the experience in Wales in 1947 and this "made a good evangelist into a great one. 'My heart is so flooded with the Holy Spirit', Billy enthused on that occasion. 'I have it. I'm filled. This is the turning point of my life.'"[40] (Stuart Piggin gives a seventeen–page review of the 1959 Billy Graham Australian crusade, and strongly affirms that it met all the criteria of a genuine revival.)[41]

I mentioned earlier a possible misunderstanding which I have sometimes heard from inquirers: "My experience has to be the same as someone else's, or it isn't the real thing." This is an error because God has made us all uniquely different. He deals with us according to our personality, and the situation we are in at the moment. To seek an experience like another's, is to violate 2 Corinthians 10:12 by comparing ourselves with others, and to miss the beauty of God's individual care for us. It can also suggest that the focus of our seeking, is the *experience*, when the real issue is seeking *Him*, being flooded with his grace and goodness—to love him supremely.

Even though I have listed many testimonies of outstanding Christians, it should be abundantly clear from the above that God has dealt *very differently* with each one. Further, he will no doubt do so in our own day, till Jesus returns. Another aspect to note from these encouraging words is that some only became aware that the wonderful change had taken place *after* it had happened, when they were looking back on their journey.

In Genesis 26:15 we read that the Philistines had stopped up the wells which Abraham had made. His son, Isaac, dug them again. We have just read of people in days past who shaped history, but what was their secret? My purpose in this book is to identify the steps *we* can follow—a bit like Isaac.

> The real issue is seeking *Him*, being flooded with his grace and goodness— to love him supremely.

---

[40] William Martin, *A Prophet with Honor*: The Billy Graham Story, 98f., quoted by Piggin, *Firestorm of the Lord*, 99.
[41] Piggin, *Spirit of a Nation*, 154–171.

Chapter 4

The Heart of the Problem—Our Inner Civil War

When we start thinking about being filled with the Holy Spirit and consider what God does in making us like Himself, both at conversion and in this deeper work, we face a major challenge: our self-centredness.

The problem is that even though we are changed at conversion, our 'old' self still wants to assert itself. We soon discover a civil war raging inside us—the guerrilla forces of sin battling against the government forces of King Jesus! A fundamental part of becoming a Christ-follower involves acknowledging that Jesus is now the King, the Lord, the Boss of our lives.

The main issue

Lewis Smedes tells of a woman in a prisoner-of-war camp watching a Nazi guard beating her friend. She felt rage and anger rising and was suddenly stopped by a surprising thought: "Remember, there is also a Nazi in you."[1] The truth is we must face the reality that the self-centredness which lies deep within us all, under certain circumstances, could make us capable of such cruelty, and worse. If only our self-centredness was like a fire we could just locate and extinguish, or like an aching tooth we could have extracted, the task would be much simpler. Paul spoke of this in Romans 6 and 7. Consider especially Romans 6:12–13. Notice the verbs in these verses "do not let sin reign..." "do not present your members..." "present yourselves..." All are *commands*, and all indicate our responsibility as a Christian. There is something we can discipline ourselves *not* to do, and something we are to discipline ourselves *to* do. Once we become aware of this, we start to notice

---

[1] Gordon MacDonald, *Rebuilding Your Broken World* (Nashville, TN: Oliver Nelson, a Division of Thomas Nelson Inc., First British Edition, 1988), 96.

how often the New Testament encourages and commands Christians to accept *their* responsibility for living in a way that pleases the Lord.

When we attempt alone, to deal with past patterns of bad behaviour, we rely on our will-power and determination. We identify the area of concern and determine never to do it again. There are several reasons why this approach will usually fail.

Habits are part of how we live in this world and changing one will usually involve several weeks of deliberate self-discipline during which familiar friends, smells and places, serve to remind us of how it used to be. It is so hard. Ask the alcoholic or drug addict how difficult it can be. Romans 7 speaks to this. Paul explains there is an inner struggle with the desire to do what is right because the Holy Spirit is in us prompting and guiding us but at the same time there is a struggle within because our old ways still have a hold on us. Secondly there are evil spirits, sometimes inherited, who are active in the battle (Ephesians 6:10–20) and where they can, they will make it harder. We may need special prayer in this area.

> The New Testament encourages and commands Christians to accept *their* responsibility for living in a way that pleases the Lord.

Further, our emotional energy is involved and it is limited, so we will likely slip back into old ways when we are tired or discouraged. In fact, the bad habit has more power because every time we think about what we are *not* going to do the old memories rear their ugly heads at the reminder. Even if we can make it for a time, sooner or later there will be the unguarded moment and we will be 'sunk'. Because of life's hurts, many of us have a residue of bitterness which can explode in a second, given the right provocation. Friends may say, "count to ten to give yourself time", but they do not understand. The trigger is set for an instant response and we find ourselves embarrassed and humiliated.

When we see we have failed, we tend to feel the tide will overwhelm us. We may have started the day with devotions and felt fairly confident, but before too long, there is trouble. Along comes someone we don't like, or a nice juicy temptation, and before we know it, we are discouraged and deflated. That is when the following verse becomes significant:

> No temptation has overtaken you except such as is common to man; but God *is* faithful, who will not allow you to be tempted beyond what you are able, but with the temptation will also make the way of escape, that you may be able to bear *it.²*

A word of encouragement

One of the most helpful pieces of advice I received along the way in this regard was, "Cheer up; the struggle is a sign of life. Any dead fish can float with the tide! Before you became a Christian, those things were not an issue. Something really has happened to make you aware of this issue in your life." However, Paul goes on in Romans 8 to speak of a new factor—the law of the Spirit of life in Christ Jesus. But what does that mean? I am to live a life in balance, by both maintaining my guard against temptation, and also keeping my trust in God's power.

> Cheer up; the struggle is a sign of life. Any dead fish can float with the tide!

Think for a moment of a hot air balloon. While we are in the basket, the higher law of thermodynamics overcomes the lower law of gravity. The law of gravity is still operating as we will discover if we step out of the basket, but while we are in there, the higher law wins. Similarly, we are in Christ and so, my focus must remain on relating to and pleasing Him, and being filled with the Holy Spirit. The law of the Spirit of life in Christ Jesus sets us free from the law of sin and death. There is no place for us to just sit back and coast.

Jerry Bridges comments:

> So we see that God has made provision for our holiness. Through Christ He has delivered us from sin's reign so that we now can resist sin. But the responsibility for resisting is ours. God does not do that for us. To confuse the potential for resisting (which God provided) with the responsibility for

---

² 1 Corinthians 10:13.

resisting (which is ours) is to court disaster in our pursuit of holiness.[3]

I need to recognise that God has made it possible for people to have a relationship with Him as His children. In my own life, He has stirred me to repent and brought me into His family by the Holy Spirit. Further, He continues to alert me to areas that are displeasing to Him and damaging to me in my Christian life. Always, He is leading me towards a closer walk with Him that will be satisfying and fruitful. At every stage, I am in His care and dependent on His strength and support. Further, I need to recognise the provisions He has made for my spiritual growth and development. I must nourish my relationship with Christ to allow His power to flow through me.

> I must starve myself of those things
> that weaken me spiritually.

Before embarking on a road trip there are some things we can do to prepare for the journey—like filling up the car tank with fuel, checking oil, tyres and so on. Similarly, our Christian journey is served well with preparation and 'nourishment' for Spiritual growth. One thing is certain: If we think things will change as we just drift along, saying the occasional prayer or doing a good deed, we are naively missing the lesson to be learned from those who have really made a difference in our world. The following is not a list of 'musts' to be followed 'religiously', but ways others have been helped. It is not a legalistic regimen, but rather a pattern.

- *Privately*: praying, reading, meditating on, and memorizing the Bible (John 17:17); studying Christian literature and resources; choosing carefully the music I let run through my mind, and the things I think about. Imagine crossing a clear sparkling lake in a motor boat. Then come back slowly in a glass bottomed one. Studying the Bible systematically is like the latter as we get a clearer view of the beauty beneath the surface.
- *With other Christians*: by meeting in a small group for accountability and enjoying their support (Ecclesiastes 4:10–12), as well as worshipping and praising God (Hebrews 10:25)

---

[3] Jerry Bridges, *The Pursuit of Holiness* (Colorado Springs, CA: NavPress, 1978), 60.

when my church gathers week by week. It has become acceptable to just give God an 'hour of worship' each week, but scripture speaks of one *day* in seven as His. So, my routine includes attending weekly worship, twice if possible, and careful use of the rest of the day, and mid-week small group as a *priority*.

Steps we can take

As well as nourishing my faith, I must starve myself of those things that weaken me spiritually. For example: ungodly internet sites, movies and television programs that do not strengthen me in the things of God; music with words that violate biblical standards and values; unwholesome magazines. Paul teaches this 'nourish the good, starve the bad' principle in most of his letters (for example: Philippians 4, Colossians 3, Ephesians 4 and 5). One preacher spoke of two dogs and asked which one wins the fight? "The one that gets fed" is the correct answer.

When I am asked by earnest seekers why they are not having success in overcoming sin, my questions focus on the *nourish / starve* principle. Paul speaks of *sowing* and *reaping* (Galatians 6:7–9). The devotional exercises mentioned above are effectively the 'sowing' part, as we till the soil, fertilize and plant good seed. The 'reaping' will follow as long as the 'weeds' are not allowed to grow. If you want to have a verdant garden, you learn to love flowers and hate weeds.

> If you want to have a verdant garden,
> you learn to love flowers and hate weeds.

However, when we despair of the capacity of our human powers of will and determination to accomplish inner transformation, we are open to a wonderful new discovery. The strength to change is a gift from God to be graciously received. The needed change within us is God's work, not ours. Since the need is for an inside job, and God alone can work from the inside, there is hope. This issue for Christians is the reason I have written this book, devoting the next chapter and much of Part 3 to the issue. As part of understanding this process, it will be helpful to compare the initial process of becoming a Christian, with the ongoing process of becoming *all* God wants us to be.

Comparing conversion with a life of obedience (consecration)

Although our experiences of conversion vary greatly there are common strands which reflect the Bible teaching on the process of becoming a Christian.[4] They begin with:

- *Repentance*: Acknowledging that we are selfish and have been trying to run our own lives independently of God, and that this rebellion is self-destructive and damaging.

- *Commitment*: Admitting our own sin and asking Christ to become Resident in us and to take the throne of our lives to make us new people, starting on the inside.

- *Acceptance by faith of what He has done*: Accepting by faith that He did on the cross what we could not do (that is, please God 100 percent). It is this faith or trust, that God accepts rather than a perfect performance, which we could not deliver (cf. Mark 1:15, Acts 2:38). This flows on to self-discipline; maintaining my relationship with Him in the ways outlined above.

The experience of a radiant character has the same common strands:

- *Repentance*: Sorrow for those pockets of sin and self-centredness that remain after conversion. God uses life's experiences to help us identify them. We thought all was surrendered to Him at conversion, so this painful process is necessary to free us from the remaining shackles of sin.

- *Full consecration*: Admitting our own selfishness and asking Christ, Who is already the Resident, to become the President in us and to take the throne of our lives in order to make us new people, starting on the inside.

- *Acceptance by faith of what He has done*: The cross holds the key to our further release as we by faith accept that we are crucified with Christ (Romans 12:1–2, Acts 26:18, Galatians 2:20). Then letting this flow on to self-discipline; maintaining, my relationship with Him as He lives in me through an ordered routine.

---

[4] This is not about the *content* of belief. That is already covered in Chapter 2.

Chapter 5

What Is Repentance and Why Does it Matter?

Dietrich Bonhoeffer, the German pastor who was martyred for his faith in 1945, is famous for the comment that "preaching forgiveness without requiring repentance, or baptism without church discipline, or communion without confession is cheap grace. It is grace without discipleship, grace without the cross, grace without Jesus Christ...."[1]

Repentance is a vital part of becoming more like Jesus. The struggle of the emerging butterfly to free itself from the cocoon, is part of a process as the fluid is forced into the wings and later hardens to become part of the wing structure. For someone to cut the outer shell, trying to help, only cripples the insect. Repentance is a process too. A conversion without the pain and sorrow for sin is incomplete, and results in 'crippled' Christians. Similarly, as we respond to the 'still small voice' bit by bit, we are completing a process that will allow us to discover a destiny under God.

Both Jesus and John the Baptist called people to "repent, for the kingdom of heaven is at hand" and when Jesus sent out the Twelve, repentance was part of their message (Mark 6:12). The preaching of the early church was the same, whether we think of Peter's message on the day of Pentecost (Acts 2:38), or Paul's in Athens (Acts 17:30).

Dealing with the past

Being freed from the guilt of past actions is an essential ingredient in having a radiant character rather than continuing under a load of guilt, which will be evident to everyone. It is like the long-buried land mines (left over from wars). The surface seems innocent enough but suddenly and unexpectedly there is an explosion and someone can be irreparably damaged. I have observed a parallel in ministry. The young bride-to-be is asked whether she

---

[1] https://www.goodreads.com/author/quotes/29333.Dietrich_Bonhoeffer—quoting from *The Cost of Discipleship*, published in 1937.

would like her marriage to be like that of her parents. Her facial expression changes, as the pain suddenly rises of memories, which will ruin her relationships if not dealt with. Memories of mistreatment, or molestation may go undealt with for years but remain *alive* until forgiven and released. Clearly the victim is innocent of the aggression, but along with learning how to forgive the offender, she needs to identify her own suppressed anger and bitterness, and seek forgiveness for it.

Repentance is not just being sorry

I well remember an occasion when I had to discipline a child, and I then told him he should apologize. He dutifully obeyed, but then I paused, softened my voice and said, "Hey, what are you sorry for?" He replied, "I'm sorry you got mad." I was in fact teaching him to lie! There was no repentance, simply unhappiness at the result. One adult, in a moment of transparency on the subject of his gambling addiction, was asked what he was sorry for, and he replied, "I'm sorry that gambling is wrong." This is not repentance, it is just sadness for being in trouble.

Whether through a scripture verse, a song, a sermon, or a chance remark, when God confronts me about something in my life that displeases Him my proper response is repentance. It is not just being sorry for the consequences or even greatly distressed and remorseful (like Judas). Rather, it is a determination to avoid that situation again and taking whatever steps I can, to follow through on my new direction.[2] As DeNeff comments, "[Repentance] is neither sorrow without change, nor change without sorrow. It is sorrow with *intent to change*."[3] It is passing from unconscious depravity to conscious depravity and facing up to our deepest need.

I am a great fan of Bill Bright and I thank the Lord for the way he summarised the gospel in a simple set of four spiritual laws. I have used them many times in sharing my faith, and it has been a thrill to pray with people as they invited Christ into their lives. On a big picture level, Steve DeNeff cites USA church statistics which show that of those people claiming to be converted, only a small minority

---

[2] The prodigal is an excellent example (Luke 15:11–24).
[3] Steve DeNeff, *Whatever Became of Holiness?* (Indianapolis, IN: Wesley Press, 1992), 44.

attends church.[4] While obviously, church membership is not everything, it *is* part of the whole of commitment, since the church is God's idea. It is not essential to becoming a Christian.[5] On the other hand, DeNeff's statistics do show that something is too often lacking. At times, I wonder whether some well-meaning believers, in trying to make it as easy as possible for others to become Christians, have just summarized it as "receive Christ", based on John 1:12. No doubt they want to help, but if what we share neglects the truth of repentance, then it is not the gospel and there will be no desire for real change.

> [Repentance] is neither sorrow without change, nor change without sorrow. It is sorrow with *intent to change.*
>
> - DeNeff -

When I was teaching at a college in Switzerland, we had many nationalities present, and I was interested to notice that the Russian Christians spoke of "when I repented" rather that our usual phrase "when I received Christ". I think they showed a healthy grasp of a vital aspect. Personally, I have found John White's insights in *Changing on the Inside*[6] very helpful in my own journey, and ministry, because the need for repentance is part of my experience too. It is more than being sorry for the *consequences* of our action. It is not unlike a visit to the dentist with a lost filling. First the problem tooth needs to be identified, prepared and cleaned out, which may involve drilling, then it can be refilled with a substance to make it complete again. Some people will put up with a fair amount of pain before they act, but the end result is always worth it.

---

[4] Ibid., 45.

[5] However, I also believe every believer needs to become committed to a group of Christ-followers for personal growth as well as ministry to the other Christians. Our culture calls that a local church.

[6] John White, *Changing on the Inside—The Keys to Spiritual Recovery and Lasting Change* (Guilford, Surrey: Eagle, 1991). I cannot too highly recommend White's book for further study. It is the best treatment of repentance I have ever read.

Moving in harmony with the Holy Spirit

The process of repentance involves two parts, the Holy Spirit and the Christian. I'm no carpenter, but it did not take me long to learn that when planing a piece of timber, you plane *with* the grain not against it. I observe the same when a sailor steers his vessel—it is moving *with* the wind, just as a skier co-operates, as it were, *with* the snow fall and the slope as he descends the mountain. When I interact with a client as a counsellor, or with an audience as a preacher, it is two-way. I offer comment and they mentally respond with 'I'll think about that', or 'yep', or 'no way'. It is not all *active* with my telling, or all *passive* with their just sitting and soaking like a sponge. Rather, they are part of the whole process of communication.[7] Repentance is like that. It is an interpersonal affair, and one that essentially always has to do with God *and also* with me as His child.

The Greek word for repentance means a change of mind. It is rather like making a 'U' turn from the self-centredness that is the essence of sin, to a God-centredness whereby we are 100 percent committed to pleasing Him. By responding to the promptings of the Holy Spirit, a radiant character can result. For example, when you have made things right with God and your neighbour by genuine apology and forgiveness, it makes possible a transparency which is both obvious, and appealing. It makes it safe for you to be yourself because you are not hiding anything. This can carry the anointing of the Holy Spirit and be an encouragement to others.

> The Holy Spirit works more like a 'marksman' aiming at a target with conviction than a 'shot-gun' of condemnation' approach.

There is a danger when we speak of repentance only in broad terms such as a blanket statement, "I repent of them all". We can repent of a selfish attitude, but the specific ways that it shows are one by one. (The Holy Spirit works more like a 'marksman' aiming at

---

[7] The Greek has a curious form called middle voice which has an extra benefit because it can provide for 'both–and' not (as in English,) 'either–or'. It is found in such places as John 14:6, Luke 14:31, Acts 13:48, 17:28, 1 Corinthians 6:11.

a target with conviction than a 'shot-gun of condemnation' approach.) The journey of self-discovery is a bit like peeling an onion, layer by layer with many tears! Yes, I was changed, but not changed enough. We committed those sins one by one so we need to avoid the grand-slam generalization which minimizes the specifics and thus misses the benefit and release.

My grandfather trained horses and I loved the stories of how he quietly and gradually, built a rapport with an animal so that when the time came to ride, there was a mystic union of man and beast. He did not sit astride the creature like a wooden puppet. Rather, the rider was *moving in harmony* with the animal. My farmer friends confirm that this is the secret of a comfortable ride. We must come to see, perhaps dimly at first, that we "live and move, and have our being" in God Himself, as Paul declared to the learned men of Athens (Acts 17:28). Like the horse rider, we need to co-operate with some thing or some One. The work of the Holy Spirit begins *long before* people become Christians. One beautiful hymn says it well: "He called me long before I heard, before my sinful heart was stirred...."[8] John 6:44 attests to this work of God in drawing us to himself.

> Any sense of desire for improvement,
> dissatisfaction, or desire for change, however
> vague, does not originate in ourselves. It is
> the beckoning of *divine Love* and *Longing*.

When God begins to operate in our lives, we are hardly aware that it is God with Whom we are dealing. We do not fully understand what is really happening, as certain thoughts and feelings float through our minds. We all have the choice of rejecting or responding to what is happening to us. There are stages in God's dealing with us, and they are successive ones depending on our response. That is why repentance is normally a prelude to change, and why real and lasting change must always include deep repentance. The truth is that any sense of desire for improvement, dissatisfaction, or desire for change, however vague, does not originate in ourselves. It is the

---

[8] Charles H Gabriel, *The Methodist Hymnbook* (London: Methodist Conference Office, Revised 1954), Hymn 336.

beckoning of *divine Love* and *Longing*.[9] We need to listen when it comes because scripture warns it will not persist forever (Genesis 6:3).

What relevance does repentance have for me as a Christian?

The Old Testament prophets consistently called Israel to repent and turn back to God.[10] Think also of Nineveh where Jonah preached to a heathen nation which was known for its cruelty, and he told *them* to repent. Later came John the Baptist, Jesus and the apostles, and early in the book of Revelation there are some letters to churches, where Jesus is calling on most of them to repent (Revelation 2–3 and Titus 2:11–12). Obviously, it is relevant for today's Church.

Our Western society has taught us to take a pride in our appearance, skills, and performance, with the result that we fail to see pride for the evil it is. Some of the most religious, the most upright and even 'spiritual' people in the world are exceedingly proud.[11] But pride makes us, like Satan, an enemy of God. In the book of Proverbs, we are told that "Everyone proud in heart, is an abomination to the Lord" (Proverbs 16:5). Is it possible that religious people could be displeasing to God? Yes. Consider who were the strongest opponents of the ministry of Jesus. The theme of God's hatred of religious pride continues all through the Bible. "Because pride is such a major element in evil, repentance often begins with the painful awareness of how great our pride is."[12]

We like to *work* our way out of the mess we have made. Make a pilgrimage, donate some money, sacrifice something—*anything* to say we have somehow made up for it and save face. Thus, our starting point in the quest for freedom from self-centredness is to *realise* that we are proud. Pride fosters evil because pride flows from comparing ourselves with others (so we can feel superior). Our Lord was very much at ease with rogues, tax collectors, harlots, and the

---

[9] I'm using the term 'preparing grace' because it makes clear that conversion is God's work from start to finish, and there is no way we can ever claim credit for any part of it. Further comment is in Definitions at Appendix A.

[10] Consider Jeremiah and the other prophets and the way Ezra, Nehemiah, and Daniel confessed the sins of the nation.

[11] C. S. Lewis, *Mere Christianity* (London: Fontana, 1954), 108–109. The whole chapter is very insightful indeed.

[12] White, *Changing on the Inside*, 77.

poor. But what of those proud, rich religious leaders of his day? It was his confronting their pride that aroused their anger enough to make them plan to crucify Him (Matthew 21–23), and the same thing applied to Judas when Jesus rebuked his hypocritical criticism of Mary (John 12:1–8).

Pride is evil because it puts us in competition with our neighbours, even with members of our family and those we love most. Lewis points out,

Each person's pride is in competition with everyone else's pride. It is because I wanted to be the big noise at the party that I am so annoyed at someone else being the big noise.... We say that people are proud of being rich, or clever, or good-looking, but they are not. They are proud of being richer, or cleverer, or better-looking, *than others.*[13]

Children show this trait early in childhood. When other siblings arrive, they love them, but resent them. The issue, however subtle, is the desire to have all the attention of the parents for themselves. So, they enter into competition with the new arrival, and it can last for years. The unpleasant reality for us, is that pride *always* means submerged (and often disguised) antagonism and rivalry.

The heart of the matter, however, is that pride puts us into competition with God himself. Pride is only comfortable when it can *look* down on others. And one cannot look down on God. Anyone who truly enters God's *presence* knows his or her absolute smallness, absolute dependency.... No wonder we need repentance.[14]

High-profile examples of repentance

As Christians, we place great stress on conversion. This is the purpose of nearly every evangelistic presentation. There are different parts of the process; accepting the message of the gospel, and on that basis, making our own commitment to, and trust in, the person of Jesus Christ. At the heart of this is faith, which involves more than an intellectual assent to certain teaching.

John White tells the story of Chuck Colson, American President Nixon's right-hand man at the time of Watergate who ended up in jail

---

[13] Lewis, *Mere Christianity*, 107.
[14] White, *Changing on the Inside*, 79.

and later founded Prison Fellowship.[15] He outlines the moments of crisis which led up to his conversion, and affirms that "something more profound was happening. [It] is attested to by his subsequent switch in values, career, and lifestyle. A radical change was taking place in the depths of his character."[16] Describing it as being like a kind of inner earthquake, he then parallels the effect of such tremors on the landscape and adds: "However, without repentance—that is, without this type of mysterious earthquake—true faith is not possible. The earthquake of repentance is the doorway to faith and to behaviour change. It is the beginning of true enlightenment."[17]

> Something more profound was happening. [It] is attested to by his subsequent switch in values, career, and lifestyle

White also quotes Dr Leo Alexander, who worked with Leon Jaworski at the Nuremburg War Crimes Tribunal:

> Whatever proportion these crimes finally assumed, it became evident to all who investigated them that they had started from small beginnings ... merely a subtle shift in the attitude of physicians. It started with the acceptance of the attitude ... that there is such a thing as life not worthy to be lived.... Gradually the sphere of those to be included in this category was enlarged to encompass the socially unproductive, the ideologically unwanted, the racially unwanted, and finally all non-Germans.[18]

There is hope

We need to beware of the way the enemy starts small and lets evil gradually increase, rather like the person who thinks a little bit of pornography doesn't matter, when it does—the brain is actually damaged.[19] Huddleston quotes "an article from The Witherspoon

---

[15] Ibid., 20–35.
[16] Ibid., 33.
[17] Ibid., 34.
[18] Ibid., 63.
[19] Brad Huddleston, *Digital Cocaine* (Vereeniging: Christian Art Publishers, 2016), 73.

Institute titled *The New Narcotic*, It compared how Internet pornography addiction is similar to cocaine and heroin addiction combined."[20]

The gospel is called Good News because there is hope. God has provided for reconstruction and healing of inner wounds, recycling them to become equipment for ministry, bringing a fresh sense of freedom and release, as well as a new foundation on which to build a better tomorrow.

Phillip Yancey in his book, *What's So Amazing About Grace*, refers to the account of the woman taken in adultery (John 8) and comments that: "Jesus replaces the two assumed categories, righteous and guilty, with two different categories: sinners who admit and sinners who deny. The woman caught in adultery helplessly admitted her guilt. Far more problematic were people like the Pharisees who denied or repressed guilt."[21] That is always a timely word for us—especially when we are seeking to serve others. We must guard against any sense of superiority which would nurture our pride. Whitefield observing a man on the way to the gallows made the famous comment, "There, but for the grace of God, go I."

The Old Testament prophets called on God's people to repent in the face of their sins. Those who preached personally identified with the sinfulness of God's people, stating *"we* have sinned" when confessing them to the Lord.[22] Today we live in a time of peace and prosperity, but our nation has forgotten God. This was the diagnosis of the tragedy of Russia's collapse, as reported by Solzhenitsyn.[23] Amazingly that nation's leaders shared with an American delegation in 1991 that the way back included 'repentance'.[24] As a people, we in the West have sinned with our crass materialism, our idolizing of sex, and the use of pornography even by some Christians, treating sport with religious fervour, as well as our neglect of worshipping the Lord, as His due. The next generation is poorly taught the

---

[20] http://www.thepublicdiscourse.com/2013/10/10846/ quoted by Huddleston, *Digital Cocaine*, 73–74.

[21] Philip Yancey, *What's So Amazing About Grace?* (Grand Rapids, Michigan: Zondervan Publishing House, 1997), 182.

[22] Ezra 9, 10, Nehemiah 1, 9, Daniel 9, Ezekiel 18, 22, Esther 4 called for fasting, and the other prophets.

[23] Phillip Yancey, *Praying with the KGB* (Portland OR: Multnomah Press, 1992), 89.

[24] Ibid., 32.

scriptures, and evolution has replaced for many, the idea of God as deserving respect and obedience as our Creator. We have not made enough disciples. It is time for us as His people to repent and seek the Lord to 'heal our land' (2 Chronicles 7:14). Ezekiel 37, the picture of revival comes right after 36:25–27, the message of a clean heart which is the focus of this book. There is hope, but we *are* called to repent.

> A radiant character is a
> precious jewel, and like most
> gems it is created under
> pressure, over time.

Some years ago, Michelangelo's famous sculpture of the body of Christ in the arms of Nicodemus, the *Pieta*, was seriously damaged when a crazed madman broke through the barriers and attacked it with a hammer. The world of art was horrified. However, a gifted artist completed repairs so that only an expert can tell where the damage was. This is a picture of what our dear Lord does with a life fully yielded to Him. Interestingly, the man doing the repairs was required to spend considerable time preparing, by studying the life of Michelangelo as part of getting himself ready for the task. Demanding, yes, but eminently worthwhile.

A radiant character is a precious jewel, and like most gems it is created under pressure, over time.

PART 2: **THE TRUTH**

Insights from God's Perspective—The Scriptures

I well recall reading of a conversation between an astronomer and a preacher, in which the former declared that he had a simple summary of theology: "Do good, and love your neighbour as yourself." The reply he received was insightful. "Yes, I have a simple summary about astronomy too: Twinkle, twinkle little star." The subject before us deserves deeper, foundational thinking than just clustering a few ideas, even if they are true. We must be sure the foundation is faithful to scripture.

This part of the book is dealing with the teaching of the Bible, and in particular the passages that make it clear that a radiant character is possible because of God's enabling.

Chapter 6

The teaching of the Bible about a godly life has various aspects:

- We can be blameless without being faultless.
- Intentional and unintentional sins—There is a difference between a sin we *know* is wrong, and one of which we are not yet aware. Understanding this is liberating.
- Scripture addresses the place of our motives.
- The Bible affirms repeatedly that purity of heart is in the present tense.
- We must be sure that our definition of sin is biblical—great news.
- Believing it *is possible* to have a radiant character.
- Love for God is the key in both the Old and New Testaments.
- We need to abide in that Love.

Chapter 7

An Expanded Horizon—moving to maturity:

- The dimension of *maturity* which moves beyond attitude to character.
- How to be filled with the Holy Spirit. What steps do we need to take?
- Why is there usually a delay between conversion and this deeper work?
- What does it mean "to be perfect, even as our heavenly Father is perfect?"
- What can we learn from the monastic movement and their three famous vows?
- The problem of temptation regarding the holy life, including a look at why God allows it.
- The importance of forgiveness, including powerful stories.
- A nutshell summary.

Chapter 6

The Teaching of The Bible about a Godly Life

The promises of Scripture

I remember exactly where I was sitting in 1970 when I first read Thomas Cook's little book *New Testament Holiness.* He was a preacher who is reported to have seen over 100,000 people come to faith preaching the message he was sharing (the message of the book you are reading). The opening chapter of his book began with the following heading:

Blameless not faultless

What a discovery that was to me. From that day on, I have watched for the use of the word *blameless* as I have read scripture, and been consistently encouraged.

> I have watched for the use of the word *blameless* as I have read scripture, and been consistently encouraged.

A close friend was enjoying time with his young daughter in the backyard one afternoon when the front door bell rang. He said, "You hold the hose and water the garden, while daddy goes to the door." When he returned, the girl was nowhere to be seen and the hose went through the door of his study which was located in a former car garage near the back fence. He found her hosing his library and explained her action with these words "Daddy, your books were dusty and I was cleaning them for you!" He spent the afternoon drying them out before putting them away. Clearly, in her childish innocence, she was not faultless, but blameless.

Our heavenly Father looks not only at *what* we do, but *why* we do it. This touches on our *motive* and gives us great hope. Jesus pointed to the matter of heart attitude in Matthew 5:6 and 8, and Peter referred to it when reflecting on the first Pentecost (Acts 15:8). As we discovered in Chapter 2, there was a time frame between Resurrection Day and Pentecost. It is also true for us when we make that total commitment to living a life pleasing to God (during which we discovered the deeper issue of our inner civil war). We must also remember the importance of the growth both before and after. Scripture implies that as far as possible, our development will take place largely as part of a community of faith.

Once we can understand this truth that blamelessness is possible, and the evidence to support it, we can then go on to seek its fulfilment in our lives. Being holy does not exempt us from making mistakes. While we are in this body, we will be subject to errors, weaknesses and sickness. But we can be free from sin, which is the wilful disobedience of God's known laws. Sin does not reside in the body but in the will. When we do not defy God wilfully, we are blameless.

Naturally, this blamelessness is not an excuse for being lazy or slack in Christian growth, and in the pursuit of being the best we can be for God. It is okay for a young child to spill milk accidentally at the table and there is no need of punishment, but if a 12-year-old has been warned about 'being silly at the table' and spills his drink, that is another matter. Rather, we are to be fully committed to pleasing God and diligently available for Him to use. It is significant that on at least one occasion *after* Pentecost Peter needed correcting, and was rebuked by Paul (Galatians 2:11–14). In Ephesians 1:4, Paul mentions God's purpose in choosing His people, that they "should be holy and without blame before Him in love."

Watchman Nee, the great Christian leader in China, believed the church needed to go 'underground' when the Communists began to legislate about Christianity and what sermons the pastors were permitted to preach. On the other hand, many leaders stayed in the 'above ground' church which the government endorsed. Here is an example of Christians taking two different courses of action, on the same issue, but both seeking to please God.

Scripture shows repeated instances of heroes and heroines of the faith who were described implicitly or explicitly as blameless, including Noah (Genesis 6:9), Abraham (Genesis 17:1), Joseph (Genesis 39 to 45), the two spies (Joshua, 2:17–19), Job repeatedly (Job 1:1,8, 2:3, 9:21), Daniel (Daniel 6:4–5 and 21) and Zechariah and Elizabeth (Luke 1:6). Paul spoke often of the need for leaders in the early church to be blameless (1 Timothy 3:2, 3:10, 5:7, Titus 1:6). He sometimes linked it with living righteously in view of Christ's return, when our blamelessness will be apparent to all (1 Corinthians 1:8, Philippians 1:9–11, 2:15–16, Colossians 1:22, 1 Thessalonians 3:13, 5:23). Further, Peter speaks of the believers to whom he wrote as blameless (2 Peter 3:14).

Unintentional sins

The Bible repeatedly says that there is a difference between a sin we *know* is wrong, and one which we have not yet learned about. See, for example, Numbers 15:22–31, where God provides a way of escape for the one who sins without malice or intent (vs. 22–29), yet He treats severely the one who sins brazenly and flagrantly without regard for God's Word (vs. 30–31). It is a mistake to equalise all transgression, unintentional or otherwise. To claim that 'sin is sin' reflects a failure to recognise that God *also* looks at the motives of the heart.

This aspect touches on the issue of conscious versus unconscious sins. This second category is very clearly identified in the writings of Moses, and again throughout the Bible. The transgression is clearly identified as still being wrong, and so an offering is prescribed to make the worshipper right with God. The first mention is in Leviticus 4:2,13–14, 22, 27 plus 5:15 and 17. Note how the context repeatedly declares it is to be acted upon *when they become aware it is sin.* This is clearly reaffirmed in Numbers 15:22–27, Joshua 20:3, Ezekiel 45:20, Hebrews 9:7, and James 4:17.

God does not expect us to confess something we do not know is wrong. That would be absurd. The good news for the Christian is that the death of Christ on the cross has made atonement for such and there is no need for us to be troubled with false guilt. This does not mean we do not care, as we are to strive to live in obedience to the teaching of scripture. As we discover another area to be corrected, we then confess, and change by the power of the Holy Spirit.

Unintentional sins are equally wrong but are not equally harmful as they do not have the force of malicious intent.

Thus, there is great hope for the Christian, as we do not have to worry about whether or not, we have unknowingly committed a sin which is displeasing to God. If so, God will bring it to our notice— maybe by a sermon, a book, the words of another, or even sense that the behaviour is displeasing to God. It is liberating to know that we can live with a clean heart even though we are still learning and growing.

Our motives

We humans constantly struggle with this issue, because we are well practised in having mixed motives. There is both the reason which we tell people, and the *real* one. Contrast Judas' harsh criticism of Mary, and his real reason, as indicated by John (John 12:4–6). Our word 'hypocrite' comes from the Greek dramas where the actor wore a mask as part of the play—a 'cover up' as it were. We do well to remember that the Lord looks on the heart and knows our innermost thoughts. How wonderful, for the person whose wholehearted desire is to please Him.

> God does not expect us to confess
> something we do not know is wrong.
> That would be absurd.

Consider the following scriptures from the New Living Translation:

- Proverbs 16:2: "People may be pure in their own eyes but the Lord examines their motives."
- Proverbs 21:2: "People may think they are doing what is right, but the Lord examines the heart."
- Proverbs 21:27: "God loathes the sacrifice of an evil person, especially when it is brought with ulterior motives".
- 1 Corinthians 4:5: "When the Lord comes, he will bring our deepest secrets to light and will reveal our private motives."
- 1 Thessalonians 2:4: "[God] is the one who examines the motives of our hearts."
- James 2:4: "doesn't this discrimination show that you are guided by wrong motives?"

- James 4:3: "Even when you do ask, you don't get it because your whole motive is wrong."

The law is like a photograph. It may begin to reflect God, but it is impossible to confine Him, nor can it convey the wonderful heart of love or His incredible wisdom, sovereignty, justice, or power. It is impossible to limit the Eternal to paper or stone, just as beautiful music is more than simply the score, or the world's oceans more than simply a coloured map. Even when we break the law, His image remains in us and we can return, apologize (confess) and resume the warmth of our precious relationship. Clearly, it is possible to do the right thing for the wrong reasons, and vice versa. It is reassuring to know that God judges righteously on the basis not just of *what* we do, but *why* we do it. This leads naturally into the next area.

> God judges righteously on the
> basis not just of *what* we do,
> but *why* we do it.

Purity of heart is in the present tense

The Old Testament reference that Wesley stressed in his teaching about the holy life[1] was Ezekiel 36:25–27 which promised a *thorough* cleansing for the people of God. It is echoed in the New Testament in such places as 1 John 1:9, 2:1 and 1 John 3:2–3.

Understanding the concept of being blameless leads naturally to a discussion about purity of heart.[2] I had been studying at a college where the emphasis seemed to be that 'we sin daily in thought, word, and deed', which left me thinking that there was really no hope of any meaningful purity of heart. So, I turned to a dictionary of Bible words[3] and searched under the word 'pure'. Some verses referred to

---

[1] Albert F. Harper (General Editor), *Study Helps* contained in *The Wesley Bible—New King James Version—A Personal Study Bible for Holy Living* (Nashville: Thomas Nelson Publishers, 1990). General comment on the 30 texts Wesley used, (page 1951) as well as the footnote for Ezekiel 36:25–29), 1246.

[2] "The 'heart' being the biblical term for the personality, the unity of the self." A comment from Dr Bert Hall, Professor of Philosophy Azusa Pacific College, when reviewing the first outline of this book.

[3] W. E. Vine, *An Expository Dictionary of New Testament Words* (Old Tappan, NJ: Fleming H. Revell Company, 1940), Volume 3, 231. (All three volumes are in one binding.)

the purity of metal for the tabernacle and such like, but when it came to purity of heart, all the references are in the *present* tense. Consider the following:

Psalm 24:3–4: "Who may ascend into the hill of the Lord? .... He who *has* clean hands and a *pure* heart."

- Psalm 73:1: "Truly God is good to Israel, to such as *are pure* in heart."
- Psalm 51:10: "Create in me a *clean* heart, O God, and renew a steadfast spirit within me."
- Job 17:9: "The righteous will move onward and forward, and those with *pure* hearts will become stronger and stronger" (NLT).
- Matthew 5:8: "Blessed *are* the *pure* in heart."
- John 17:17: "Make them *pure* and holy by teaching them your words of truth" (NLT).
- 1 Timothy 1:5: "The purpose of the commandment *is* love from a *pure* heart, from a good conscience, and from sincere faith."
- 1 Timothy 3:9: "[Deacons must hold to] the mystery of the faith with a *pure* conscience."
- 2 Timothy 2:22: 'Flee also youthful lusts; but pursue righteousness, faith, love, peace with those who call on the Lord out of a *pure* heart."
- 1 Peter 1:22: "Love one another fervently with a *pure* heart."

There is a curious reference in Paul's second letter to the Corinthians where he urges *them* to do something. "Therefore, ... *let us cleanse ourselves* from all filthiness of the flesh and spirit, perfecting holiness in the fear of God" (2 Corinthians 7:1). That speaks of something *we* are to do. Remember the reminders from Jerry Bridges in Chapter 4 that the responsibility for resisting temptation is ours.

The Old Testament system focused on the sacrifice of a lamb for the sins of the worshiper, but it had to be clean. When they arrived at the temple for sacrifice, they were grubby from being in the field and the first step was to have them scrubbed clean to be suitable for offering to the Lord. God's Word, especially when read regularly, has that cleansing effect on the mind of the believer (John 15:3). When we confess, intending with God's help to stay away from that sin in the future (Psalm 51:1–14), the Holy Spirit strengthens us in our resolve. Later in the New Testament John writes, "Everyone who has this hope in Him, *purifies* himself, just as He is pure" (1 John 3:3). Again, scripture is speaking of something that involves our 'decision of the will' to take action, and the implication is that this will make a difference. That is very encouraging but there is more to come.

Definition of 'sin'

I was sharing with some teens after school, and one youth put it this way: "God, You can run the universe but *I* will run me." Another said, "Sin is treating God as a nothing." This independent way of thinking will invariably lead to attitudes and actions that are damaging both to ourselves and to others. They are in fact sins.

Obviously, the violation of the precepts and instructions of Mosaic law was a starting point toward the concept for Jews, but clearly Jesus is teaching a more all-encompassing view in the Sermon on the Mount. There is more to pleasing God than what the Scribes and Pharisees declared. Consider his statement: "Unless your righteousness exceeds the righteousness of the scribes and Pharisees, you will by no means enter the kingdom of heaven (Matthew 5:20).

When I was teaching High school, the rule was 'no one goes into the class room during lunch hour'. One day I stayed back doing some marking. A lad came along and was partially entering when he saw me and did a sudden little twist-twirl and kept walking. A short time later, as I was at the far end of the veranda I glanced back to see another entering. The difference 'boiled down' to which one had the opportunity. Both had the desire to break the rule but only one had a chance. For someone to be good only when there is no opportunity for sin is not the same as holiness.

A famous newspaper ran a competition concerning what's wrong with the world. G. K. Chesterton, the English writer, had the shortest submission. He wrote: "Sir, I am." We are too ready to see sin as something out there. This issue of *attitude* has its roots early in the Old Testament. Think of Samuel's solemn words to Saul: "Rebellion is as the sin of witchcraft" (1 Samuel 15:23). Similarly, in the Sermon on the Mount Jesus gives a more searching test when he says *wanting* to sin (Matthew 5:28), constitutes a violation. The only difference in such cases between committing the offence and legal innocence is a matter of who had the opportunity. How encouraging that the Lord searches our hearts and that an obedient attitude is more important that just keeping a written law as interpreted by religious leaders. Wesley's definition of sin helps greatly: "A wilful transgression of a known law of God."

His mother, Susanna, added another important insight: "Whatever weakens your reason, impairs the tenderness of your conscience, obscures your sense of God, or takes off the relish of spiritual things ... that thing is sin to you, however innocent it may be in itself."[4] Part of how we decide whether an action is sinful or harmful, is its effect on our walk with God.

> Part of how we decide whether an action is sinful or harmful, is its effect on our walk with God.

G. Campbell Morgan comments,

Sin as actual transgression in the past must be pardoned, and sin as a principle of revolution within must be cleansed.... When we look at Him again, and say, 'Master, there is more to in Your cross than pardon,' then He makes us conscious of His power to cleanse.[5]

This is the deeper work we all need.

Believing it *is* possible to have a radiant character

Paul's prayer for the Thessalonians has much to teach us in this regard. "Now may the God of peace Himself sanctify you completely; and may your whole spirit, soul, and body be preserved blameless at the coming of our Lord Jesus Christ. He who calls you is faithful, who also will do it" (1 Thessalonians 5:23–24). I notice it is a prayer which Paul expected to be answered, which reminds me that God *does* want us to be fully set apart for Him. Martin Luther translated it

---

[4] This insightful comment was in a letter she sent him in June 1725 in reply to his question regarding the difference between sins and 'innocent pleasures'. Quoted by Robert G. Tuttle, Jnr., *John Wesley: His Life and Theology* (Grand Rapids. Zondervan Publishing House, 1978), 67.
[5] G. Campbell Morgan, *Discipleship* (London: Morgan and Scott Ltd., 1897), 4–5.

'through and through'.[6] The NKJV has 'sanctify you completely', and NLT says, 'holy in every way', make the meaning clear. The discovery that we can be blameless fits here along with the fact that it will be obvious to all when Jesus returns. But the verse goes on to encourage us with the reminder that this is God's work and as we are obedient to Him *He will do it*. In a world where everyone welcomes the thought that 'nobody is perfect' (a useful excuse) here is a scripture that reflects God's desire that we be the best we can be. The very presence of the prayer in scripture is a good indication that it really is possible and I would add 'incredibly liberating'. It fits well with the Hebrews benediction (Hebrews 13:20–21), that we be "complete in every good work to do His will". However often I 'mess up' and disobey the Lord, there is always the possibility of a better performance in the future after confession, which leads to serving with a clean heart even in the midst of life's muddles. We will have a closer look at what it means to be *perfect* in the next chapter.

Love for God is the key

I was reading Moses' instructions to the children of Israel just before they entered the promised land and I saw that there were blessings for obedience and punishment for disobedience, which was common practice for treaties of that day. But I was amazed to read: "This command I am giving you today is not too difficult for you to understand or perform" (Deuteronomy 30:11 NLT). So what follows was obviously possible. Then He continues with: "Choose to love the Lord your God and to obey him and commit yourself to him, for he is your life" (vs. 20 NLT).

Hence it is possible to have a pure heart even though our judgement and decisions will not always be the wisest or most clever. This holds the key, because it directs us to a relationship of love as providing the power to withstand temptation and testing. It is important to remember that Jesus told the disciples in the Upper Room that if they would 'abide in His love', they would 'keep His commandments'. That is both an instruction and a promise, and it flows on to others as radiance. When Jesus was asked one day what was the greatest commandment, He spoke in similar vein, saying "The most important commandment is this: '.... you must love the Lord your God with all your heart, all your soul, all your mind, and all

---

[6] As does the New International Version.

your strength.' The second is equally important: 'Love your neighbour as yourself.' No other commandment is greater than these" (Mark 12:29–31 NLT).

When we in the 21ˢᵗ century speak of 'falling in love', we do not even entertain the idea that it should be temporary. It jumps over the high wall of our self-centredness. We toss personal happiness aside, and place the interests of another at the centre of our being. It is a sample of what we must all become if Love Himself rules in us without a rival. It puts a whole new meaning on our concept of heaven. Glenn Clark has insightfully commented: "Finding no other way of showing man what heaven is like, God invented marriage." It is so true that being loved unconditionally by one's spouse is a foretaste of what it will be like to live among a community of people who love like that. It also portrays an exclusivity of loyalty which has a parallel with the gospel. The above scriptures indicate that the Lord was looking for that kind of devotion from His people and was grieved when it was diluted or betrayed. Consider the Old Testament prophet Hosea and his dramatic lived-out statement to unfaithful Israel when he married, and loved a prostitute. He then rescued her after she was in trouble again. God still seeks our love in response to His kindness, today.

> Our search for meaning will
> ultimately only be fully
> satisfied by a relationship with
> the ultimate One, God.

When you love someone, you delight in doing what pleases them and your love also empowers you to refrain from conduct or comment which would grieve them. There is still the freedom to do so but a more powerful motivation has been added to the equation. For the sanctified believer, there remains the freedom to sin, but now there is also a freedom and strength to say 'no'. In so many ways the search for meaning is a search for relationship, as we are made in the image of a triune God. The Father loves the Son, and the Holy Spirit, Who loves the Father and the Son—and so on. Our search for meaning will ultimately only be fully satisfied by a relationship with the ultimate One, God. This then flows on to how we relate to others here on earth, adding wonderfully to the whole of life.

A saying which always stirs me is this wise couplet: "As I look back, this is what matters; I have loved and been loved. All the rest is just background music."

We need to abide in love

How cruel it would be of God to show us the immensity of our needs, but not supply them when He has promised to do so: "My God shall supply *all* your need according to His riches in glory by Christ Jesus" (Philippians 4:19).

We Christians need to experience what we preach. Holiness must not become a mere doctrine or the lost experience of another generation. We must experience our own revival of holiness in this generation, which will thrust us out like the early Christians, burning with a holy fire within us. Then there will be power and transformation, not only in the church, but also in the world.

> How cruel it would be of God to show us the immensity of our needs, but not supply them when He has promised to do so.

Another important warning concerns the danger of hardness of heart. It can come with the weariness of ministry, when one cannot sustain the needed level of emotional energy, and begins to harden into cynicism and a tendency towards condemnation. One of the reasons we are allowed to struggle with temptation is not just to encourage us to cling to God, but also to remind us how hard it is to be done with sin. Hence, we need to stay close to the Lord since His great reservoir of love is available to us, and let it continue to flow on to others through our personality and interaction.

John 15:1–12 records Jesus' words stressing the importance of abiding. Just as the branch needs to stay in vital union with the vine, so we need to remain in Him. It is our relationship that must be sustained and tended carefully—but oh, how worthwhile it is to do so. In the next chapter, we will look at the letter to the Ephesians which clearly links a fullness of love with the work of the Holy Spirit.

The Old Testament promises a new covenant which we are told in the book of Hebrews was instituted when Jesus offered Himself as the final sacrifice for all sin (Hebrews 9:11–15). This grand truth also gives us great hope in the quest for holiness. Imagine how comforting the following verses were for the Jewish exiles, and are for us as Christians.

> Behold, the days are coming, says the Lord, when I will make a new covenant with the house of Israel and with the house of Judah—not according to the covenant that I made with their fathers in the day that I took them by the hand to lead them out of the land of Egypt, My covenant which they broke, though I was a husband to them, says the Lord.

> But this is the covenant that I will make with the house of Israel after those days, says the Lord: I will put My law in their minds, and write it on their hearts; and I will be their God, and they shall be My people. No more shall every man teach his neighbour, and every man his brother, saying, 'Know the Lord,' for they shall know Me, from the least of them to the greatest of them, says the Lord. For I will forgive their iniquity, and their sin I will remember no more (Jeremiah 31:31–34).

This passage is quoted in full in Hebrews 8:6–12, and verse 13 makes it clear that the new covenant has made the former one obsolete, growing old and ready to disappear. Also linked are Ezekiel 36:25–28 and Joel 2:28–32. Note that these scriptures include promises of a filling with God's Spirit that will make doing His will both possible and powerful.

Dr Sangster[7] tells of a friend who developed a cure for rheumatism. As word got around, he was repeatedly approached for the prescription. A little while later, he noticed that some who had secured his formula were still suffering, and on enquiry found that they had not taken it. So, he put a little heading at the top of the page: "This will do you no good—*unless you take it!*" As you read on, remember that the counsel offered in this book will do you no good unless you follow through with implementing it.

---

[7] Sangster, *The Secret of Radiant Life*, 32.

Chapter 7

An Expanded Horizon—Moving to Maturity

The Christian faith is recognised as a relationship with the Lord as we study the scriptures, hearing him speak and talking to him in prayer. The New Covenant towards which the Old Testament was moving continues and enhances the idea of knowing God as One with whom we communicate on a regular basis. Think of passages such as Exodus 33:15, Jeremiah 9:23–24, Daniel 11:32, Philippians 3:10, and our Lord's prayer in John 17:3, all accenting the importance of knowing God. This relationship is not a static thing like football goal posts. Rather it is a deepening thing like marriage, from the first infatuation onto steady continuing growth and love, like changing gears upward in a car. As Thomas Cook says, "A mother is not content that her child should be in perfect health, she longs that it may grow to perfect maturity."[1]

My observation as I study scripture and church history is that all the 'greats', including our Lord, experienced suffering, often unjustly, and that this process seems to have added character, a quality previously missing, which was essential (Hebrews 5:7). This moves beyond mere attitudes, to the mature person we are becoming. The Christian sees it as a reminder that there is a better world beyond, and that the experiences of this life are refining us into Christ's image in preparation for that wonderful day.

We need to see our motivation to please God as love, not obligation. This reminds us that our love for God is the only perfection available on this earth, which is one of love and it flows on to a perfection of *purpose*, to serve with the inner obedience of heart and will. Suppose I give my dear wife some flowers and when she says, "Thanks", I reply, "That's no big deal, I'm only doing my duty!" It spoils everything. Our relationship is more than just prescribed

---

[1] Thomas Cook, *New Testament Holiness* (Fort Washington, PA: Christian Literature Crusade, n.d.), 39.

duties and demands. It is the little extras which are expressions of love.

The problems of our journey are made worse when we compare ourselves with others. In fact, 2 Corinthians 10:12 says that to do so is not wise. This temptation is just as difficult for Christians to face—especially those earnestly desiring to be the best that they can be for God. We too easily forget that God treats each person as special and unique. There is no mass-production line here. So, the way *we* experience the fullness of the Holy Spirit will vary greatly according to our personality and circumstances at the time of our encounter with God. Some will be outgoing and exuberant, and others deeply contemplative. Both are valid and need to be appreciated.

Steps to being filled

Firstly, we need to follow protocol just as we do in other important matters. When we go to catch a plane, a hand-written page with all the needed information on it, will not do at the departure lounge, however accurate the data may be. There is a proper procedure to be followed at the ticket office and then waiting to board. Similarly, there is a right way to seek God's fullness.

Secondly, scripture teaches that there is a place for *longing* to be filled, a restlessness that there is still something missing. Jesus spoke in terms of hungering and thirsting after righteousness and promised that those so doing, are blessed because they will be filled (Matthew 5:6). I pray that this book will be a means of opening the door for that wonderful change for you. Remember that to fill a bottle takes time under the tap, as the water flows in, and we need to recognise that time in the presence of God is just as necessary.

As part of our preparation there is a sequence which is almost a process as we come to a willingness (sometimes even desperation), to surrender *every* area of our lives to God. It includes our past, present, future, our bodies and our minds as well as our relationships, our reputations, and our property (Romans 12:1–2). They are really all His, and need to be carefully seen as belonging to Him. Often, more time may be needed for God to show us areas not yet fully His. If this step is neglected, we may end up not overcoming, but simply ignoring sin.

Thirdly, we need to confess every known sin to God, remembering that "if we confess our sins, He is faithful and just to forgive us *our* sins and to cleanse us from all unrighteousness" (1 John 1:9). We don't need to worry about those we cannot remember because God will bring them to our mind if He wants us to deal with them.

One source of confusion for Christians is the notion that we get all we are going to get of the Holy Spirit at conversion and now it is simply a matter of growth. To understand the importance of the deeper work of the Spirit, a useful question to ask would be whether or not the Holy Spirit has all of *us*, because it is usually only as we progress along the Christian journey that we realise the unpleasant truth that there are areas of our lives which we are reluctant to surrender to His control.

Fourthly, there is the place of asking, or claiming by faith. As we have sought to be obedient, repenting of known sin and forgiving those who have wronged us, then we can ask, remembering that: "If you then, being evil, know how to give good gifts to your children, how much more will *your* heavenly Father give the Holy Spirit to those who ask Him!" (Luke 11:13).

The 19th century saw a rise of preachers who stressed the concept that since the fullness of the Spirit is God's will, we can claim it any time we wish and then publicly declare, by faith, that we now have it. Some have called this 'name it and claim it' or even 'blab it and grab it'. I have never been comfortable with this (especially when used by some other Christian groups today, in regard to prosperity). Sadly, some end up with a 'fake it till you make it' mindset which soon fades.

An electric light bulb is designed to give light. The shapes, intensity and sizes of bulbs all vary but each has the same basic purpose—to provide light, and needs the same basic input—power. Placed on the table alone it will not shine. You can even put it in the socket of a lamp but until the power is switched on there is no reason to expect a shining result (Acts 1:8). It is the same with us. We are made in the image of God and rescued from sin by the combination of repentance and faith. The Holy Spirit comes to be in us at conversion and then a change begins to take place, rather like a grub as it turns into a butterfly—a process called metamorphosis.

Remember the place of *loving* the Lord. When Jesus was asked by His opponents what was the greatest commandment, He spoke of loving God with our whole heart, mind and strength and our neighbour as ourselves (Matthew 22:37–40). When we love our enemies, pray for those who persecute us and bless those who curse us, we are behaving as children of our Father in heaven. The source of strength to behave in that way is our love for God, or—better still—His love in us, which flows on to our actions and the way we treat others.

I do enjoy gardening and have had a compost heap out the back in most places where we have lived. After six months or so, I could transfer it to the vegetable patch. When I shovelled the sticky black soil out for the garden, I always wore boots and they would often be very dirty indeed. What stopped me wearing them into the house? Was it my wife standing at the door with a rolling pin? Of course not. My love for her meant that out of love, I refrained from behaviour I was completely free to do. As we deepen our love for God, it can have the same effect of strengthening us to say 'no' to behaviour while the option remains wide open to us.

> Paul would never have gloried in his infirmities (2 Corinthians 12:9) if he had confused them with sin.
>
> - Purkiser et. al. -

For our sins [evil attitudes and actions] we need forgiveness; for our sin [self-centredness] we need cleansing, but for our infirmities [illness, memory failure and the like] we need help. "Paul would never have gloried in his infirmities (2 Corinthians 12:9) if he had confused them with sin, or had viewed them as an impediment to entire holiness."[2] God's purpose for us is to love Him, and each other, and to be holy. Our infirmities may be seen as the scars of sin, but no guilt is involved. This includes sickness, errors of judgement, and mistakes. It is not a sin to forget something! So we have every reason to be glad.

---

[2] W.T. Purkiser, et al. *God, Man, & Salvation* (Kansas City, MI: Beacon Hill Press.1977), 472.

Why a delay?

In Chapter 2 when speaking of the fullness of the Holy Spirit, one question which was raised is "Why is there a delay between conversion and this deeper work?" This deserves further comment. There were experiences Jacob went through before and after his Bethel encounter (Genesis 28:10–22), and likewise before he faced a greater threat at Peniel (Genesis 32:22–31). It is not unlike the delay for the disciples between Easter, and their filling at Pentecost. During those days sharing life in the Upper Room they would most likely have worked through areas of past misunderstandings because we read that there was oneness on the day (Acts 2:1).[3]

The delay surfaces as we discover that our conversion did not result in an ongoing perfect performance. Our unsuccessful efforts to be 100 percent like Jesus reveal the need for a further and deeper work. The plain truth is that such a discovery usually takes time. Cornelius may seem to be an exception, but obviously had a fair measure of faith prior to Peter's visit as he is described as one who feared God (Acts 10:2), and his response to the angels also reflected it.

> Our unsuccessful efforts to be 100 percent like Jesus reveal the need for a further and deeper work.

It is significant that Reformed scholar Dr Martyn Lloyd-Jones, recognises the delay factor as to when one receives the baptism of the Holy Spirit.

These are but some examples out of many more which I could give. In all of them the point that emerges is what we have already discovered from the Scriptures themselves, that there

---

[3] Another reason for the delay in the case of the disciples, was the parallel God seems to have intended with the three great Jewish feasts. *Passover* was paralleled with our Lord's crucifixion when His shed blood as the Passover Lamb and secured our freedom from sin. The next great feast was *Pentecost* which was a harvest festival. Jesus had spoken of the "harvest being great" (Matthew 9:37). This was the beginning of the harvest of souls as 16 nationalities heard "the wonderful works of God in their own language" and 3000 were added to the church. There is also a timetable in *our* lives as God unfolds His great plan for each of us individually. Also, God is preparing for the return of Jesus, and the Feast of *Trumpets* fits there.

is this interval, as it were, between Romans 8:15 and Romans 8:16. It is to believers that this happens. 'Having believed, ye were sealed with that Holy Spirit of promise.' As it happened on the day of Pentecost to the Apostles, so it has happened to the others.

When does this happen? There are some instances in which it is almost simultaneous with conversion. Take the case of Cornelius and his household; 'while Peter was still speaking the Holy Spirit fell upon them'. But in the light of all the other examples and illustrations we realise that, even there, there must have been belief first—but the interval was a very short one. But in the vast majority of instances there is a clear interval, sometimes there is a long interval. The important principle is that the two things are always separable. And surely this is quite inevitable, for, if the Spirit confirms our own spirit, there must therefore have been something that has happened in our spirit first for the Holy Spirit to confirm. You cannot have 'the Spirit of adoption, whereby we cry, Abba, Father', without being a believer. Believing must come first. What the Spirit does is to testify with our spirit. If there was no testimony in our spirit, the Spirit could not confirm it. So it follows, of necessity, from every standpoint—from the plain teaching of Scripture, from the testimonies of men, and from an obvious deduction drawn from the very nature of what is happening—that believing must precede the testimony of the Holy Spirit.[4]

He refers to this briefly, but very clearly, in the lives of each of the following: Whitefield, Wesley, Howell Harris, Jonathan Edwards, Finney, Moody,[5] and he follows up with quotes from others, including John Owen, Thomas Brooks, Charles Simeon, and C. H. Spurgeon.[6]

When Jesus was asked for the greatest commandment (Matthew 22:36–40), He immediately went to Deuteronomy 6:5 and Leviticus 19:18. Frankly, the rest of the Old Testament unfolds the failure of God's people to obey those two, and the New Testament is about how God provided another way for the needed behavioural change

---

[4] D. Martyn Lloyd-Jones, *Romans—Exposition of Chapter 8:5–17—The Sons of God* (Edinburgh: The Banner of Truth Trust, 1974), 317–318.
[5] Ibid., 316–317.
[6] Ibid., 318–323.

to be possible. To be honest, the long history of the church has the highs of greatness and the lows of failure to follow His instructions.

However, God does not command without providing a way for us to obey that command. That is why the promise of Acts 1:8, "… you shall receive power when the Holy Spirit has come upon you …" is so important. Lloyd-Jones mentioned the baptism of the Holy Spirit which is predicted in all four gospels and in Acts 1–2. The Greek word for 'baptize' can also be used to mean 'saturate' or 'dye' a garment. The concept has a link with the Old Testament, where we read "the Spirit of the Lord came upon Gideon" (Judges 6:34).[7] The same word is used in 1 Chronicles 12:18 regarding Amasai one of King David's captains. It is thoroughly consistent with the Old Testament promises of the Holy Spirit's role in the new covenant (Joel 2:28–32).

I would rather go up a steep hill in a car than on a bike. The difference is that the former has an extra source of power than just my personal exertion. We grow in love *over time*. The delay we have just been considering allows for an increase in God's power in our lives.

> We grow in love *over time*.

How perfect are we supposed to be?

The Sermon on the Mount includes the statement that we are to be perfect, even as our heavenly Father is perfect (Matthew 5:48). What did Jesus mean? Scripture speaks thus, of Noah, and Job, (remember the references to 'blameless' in Chapter 6), and the Psalmist points us to a perfect man (Psalm 37:37). Further, Jesus' words above are in fact a command, and in Hebrews He is described as "having been made perfect through suffering". Then there is the unforgettable benediction in Hebrews 13:20–21 where the writer prays that the God of peace would make the believers "complete [perfect] in every good work to do His will …" The word translated 'perfect' (KJV) is the Greek *teleios,* which means *complete* or *'just right for the task'*, as the modern translations have it, like a key that

---

[7] The Hebrew is literally 'clothed Himself with'.

75

fits the lock, or a tradesman's tool that is just the one he needs to do the job. What a reassuring thought.

What do we learn from the monks?

The Christian church has tried many ways to solve the problem of temptation. In the final period of the Roman Empire, there was increasing disillusionment with society, and even with the institutional church, some of whose leaders had succumbed to a measure of corruption. The answer of the Monastic movement was to withdraw, usually into a community, sheltered by high walls and three famous vows—poverty, chastity, and obedience.

The fruit of this approach became all too evident. While it meant an escape for the monks, the loss of keen Christians from the local church and community in Israel and North Africa so weakened the society that it collapsed before the invading Moslems in the 7th century. Further, it didn't solve the problem for the monks because legalism and rules only handcuff sin. They do not destroy it!

In other parts of Europe, the loss of the truly devoted Christians from effective participation in daily church life allowed corruption among officials and leaders to become worse, and even the monasteries failed to avoid the problem within their own ranks. The Middle Ages saw the successive rise of new Orders, each determined to reform and to make a fresh start. Finally, a young German monk named Martin Luther, of the Augustinian Order, was protected and used by God to teach afresh the timeless truth of grace under the authority of scripture. The Protestant Reformation had begun.

Its finest expression in 17th century England came through the Puritans who sought a more biblical response to temptation than the three classic vows. Instead of a vow of poverty, the Puritans placed a stress on *industry*, and they did this because they believed in all work as sacred. They totally rejected as unbiblical the concept that any part of life was secular and thus unrelated to their Christian faith. This does not mean that they were 'workaholics' or encouraged the practice, but rather that they urged the balancing of priorities.

Instead of a vow which renounced marriage, the Puritans urged *faithfulness* within marriage (in a fashion quite different from the way the word 'puritan' is used today). They maintained a wholesome balance between unhealthy inhibitions on one hand and infidelity on the other. Further, instead of a monastic vow of obedience that renounced any power (except those in authority, of course), the Puritans urged *order*, with checks and balances, both in Church and State. In so doing they laid the foundation for the freedoms we have enjoyed in a democracy.

Richard Foster has helped us with his study of these three areas. He concludes that the 21st century calls for fresh vows in the face of gross materialism, sexual confusion, and insane clambering over each other seeking power. He urges a lifestyle totally committed *to simplicity, fidelity,* and *service.* Take a moment to reflect on these three. In his book *Money, Sex and Power,*[8] there is a helpful treatment of this theme. If you can secure a copy, review especially pages 1–15 and 247–248. Pray for your life and your church. How would it be if modern followers of Christ lived by these priorities?

Temptation and the holy life

I mentioned evangelist and author Thomas Cook earlier, and how he encouraged me, from his very first chapter explaining 'blameless but not faultless'.[9] As a young student I was so grateful and then his second chapter dealt with another topic which I wanted to understand better—the issue of temptation. His opening sentence was, "It is a mistake to suppose that there is any state of grace this side of heaven, which puts a Christian where he is exempt from temptation."[10]

Jesus Himself, beside whom none is holier, was faced with the severest of temptations from the beginning of His ministry (Matthew 4:1–11), all the way to the cross. Consider Gethsemane (Matthew 26:34–46), and the taunts of rulers (Matthew 27:41–46). There is a vast difference between sin and temptation. Temptation is not wrong; sin lies in surrendering to it. Holiness does not mean we cannot sin but that God gives us the strength to say, "no".

Have you ever wondered why God allows temptation? It seems we face it in such routine situations as deciding about program options for television, ownership of property, all the way to our relationships with others. No matter what we do, we cannot escape it. The Bible deals with temptation from the first pages of Genesis.

---

[8] Richard J. Foster, *Money, Sex & Power—The Challenge to the Disciplined Life* (London: Hodder and Stoughton, 1985).
[9] Cook, *New Testament Holiness*, 7–11.
[10] Ibid., 12.

The garden had a tree from which the happy couple were not to eat—the tree of the knowledge of good and evil.

Why God allows temptation in our world:

- There had to be an option to reject God if our *choice* to follow Him was to have any meaning. The stronger the pressure (within limits) to turn away from Him, the clearer it is, that our choice to obey is a conscious expression of loyalty.

- God is more concerned with building our character for eternity than with making us comfortable and happy in this life.

- Temptation shows us our true selves when we thought we were okay. Consider the examples of Saul, David, Esther, and Peter.

- We see our cleverness wither when confronted with our failures, and with humility we place our utter dependence on God. This drives us to prayer for God's help. Remember that Jesus included "lead us not into temptation" in the prayer He taught His followers. One person restated it as, "Please minimize the tests."

- The struggles we face with temptation develop in us sympathy for others who are under pressure. Jesus' earthly life had its testings.

There are wonderful promises we can claim:

- 1 Corinthians 10:13: "No temptation has overtaken you except such as is common to man; but God is faithful, who will not allow you to be tempted beyond what you are able, but with the temptation will also make the way of escape, that you may be able to bear it."

- Hebrews 2:18: "Since he himself has gone through suffering and temptation, he is able to help us when we are being tempted" (NLT).

- Hebrews 4:15–16: [Jesus] faced all of the same temptations we do, yet he did not sin. So let us come boldly to the throne of our gracious God. There we will receive his mercy, and we will find grace to help us when we need it" (NLT).

You may like to mark the promise and exhortation in these verses. We need to be sure we have the distinction clear between temptation and sin, especially as we see the contrast in Jesus' life.

The great Salvationist S. L. Brengle comments: "This is a world of trial, and conflict with principalities and powers, darkness and terrible evils, and the holy soul who is in the forefront of the conflict may expect the fiercest assaults of the devil, and the heaviest and most perplexing and prolonged temptations."[11]

Keith Drury's very helpful book *Money, Sex and Spiritual Power*, lists some profound and insightful thoughts on temptation. The headings below will give you a 'sneak preview' of the areas he covers:

Great temptation often follows 'spiritual highs.'
The devil tempts us at our weak points.
The mind is a battlefield.
The Bible is our weapon.
The devil doesn't give up easily.
Temptation is not sin [—yielding is].
You cast the deciding vote.[12]

> "Since he himself has gone through suffering and temptation, he is able to help us when we are being tempted".

Before leaving the subject of temptation it is important to be aware of a curious trap the devil lays— 'praying *to* the temptation'. When drawn to sin, do not focus your mind on the sin. For example, if tempted to smoke a cigarette do not keep thinking of the packet. If it is toward lust, do not let your mind dwell on the action you are resisting. If tempted to steal, do not focus on the item desired. If tempted to criticise, do not focus on the offence or an undesirable quality in the person.

---

[11] S. L. Brengle, *Heart Talks on Holiness* (https://jesus.org.uk/sites/default/files/media/documents/.../heart-talks-on-holiness.pdf), 10.

[12] Keith Drury, *Money, Sex & Spiritual Power* (Indianapolis, IN: Wesley Press, 1992), 89–95. The contents of this book are available to view at "www.drurywriting.com/keith/index.books" or it may be available in your church/college library. However, it is well worth securing your own copy.

Make a conscious effort to obey Philippians 4:8. Get your mind onto another subject. Doing so is called 'thought displacement'. Change location. Pray a short prayer for help and get going on some project or chore that needs doing. Reflect on the following three scriptures and identify the truth for the sanctified Christian: 1 Peter 5:8–9, James 4:7–8 and Ephesians 6:16.

Above all, remember that quality devotional time with God as soon as possible after rising for the day, is the best preparation for all that it holds. It is also a protection against yielding to temptation because it means we have drawn on His strength, and have focussed our mind on His truth and priorities. When we have taken His armour, including the shield of faith, we can face the day, careful but unafraid. There is a further comment on this theme in Chapter 8.

The importance of forgiveness

Since we all battle with hurts from others, a comment about forgiveness is relevant at this point.

Leonardo da Vinci had been hurt by a fellow artist and when he painted *The Last Supper*, he portrayed the man's face as Judas. Everyone who came to look at the painting who knew the man recognised him and laughed at the likeness. What a way to get even! The trouble was he could not finish the picture until he forgave the man and painted a different face.

If God can forgive *us*, we can also stop blaming ourselves. Josh McDowell quotes a director of a mental hospital who said that "half of his patients could go home if they knew they were forgiven."[13]

> If God can forgive *us*, we can also stop blaming ourselves.

Sadly, we can be harder on ourselves than God is. Forgiveness frees us from *self-preoccupation.* This positive self-image is a by-product of our pursuing the goal of knowing Christ and being conformed to His image. We must remember, that having a healthy self-image is not our goal. Knowing *Christ*, in all His fullness, is.

---

[13] Josh McDowell, *His Image, My Image—Biblical Principles for Improving Your Self-Image* (San Bernardino, CA: Here's Life Publishers, Inc. (A Campus Crusade for Christ Book), 1984), 118.

Too often we are like circus elephants tied to a bicycle chain. It is not the chain that holds him but the memory that keeps him from trying to escape. When the creature was much smaller with much less strength, it was chained, and though it tried to get free, it couldn't. Now it does not try anymore. Many people have a self-image that functions much like the chain, based on a painful childhood memory, whether from parents, teachers, or peers. It is made worse when we refuse to forgive others and thereby endanger our own eternal future (Matthew 18:23–35).[14]

The really sad part is that if we haven't forgiven and settled past hurts, the next time a similar situation arises, we will drag a negative bias in and probably cause damage— "Here we go again...."

One of the most liberating things we can do is to thank the Lord for all the experiences of our lives and the way He promised to bring good out of *all* of them. It is very healthy to begin to see ourselves as God sees us—and very liberating.

> Several centuries ago a great scholar, Morena, was forced to live as a Protestant exile. Falling seriously ill [in Italy], he was taken to a paupers' hospital. The doctors, assuming the wretched-looking man could not speak Latin, began speaking that language among themselves at his bedside. They said, "This one is going to die anyway, so let's try an experiment on this worthless creature." On hearing that, Dr Morena raised up, looked at the physicians and said, "What Jesus died for, how can you call worthless?"[15]

Luther correctly said, "God does not love us because we are valuable; we are valuable because God loves us."[16] We could well add "and enables us to love others".

In a nutshell

Being filled with the Holy Spirit is:

- Not the inability to sin, but the ability *not* to sin.
- Not freedom *from* temptation, but power to overcome temptation.

---

[14] Jesus taught us to pray "forgive us our sins, just as we have forgiven those who have sinned against us" (Matthew 6:12 NLT).
[15] McDowell, *His Image, My Image*, 121.
[16] Ibid., 120.

- Not infallible judgement, but earnest and honest endeavour to follow the higher wisdom.
- Not deliverance from infirmities of the flesh, but triumph over all bodily affliction.
- Not exemption *from* conflict, but victory *through* conflict.
- Not the end of progress, but the deliverance from standing still.
- An experience that comes to *believers* and thus *after* conversion.

As with many of Paul's letters, the foundation comes in the first half and the application builds on it. This is particularly clear in Ephesians where there is a powerful benediction at the end of Chapter 3 signalling the shift. The command to be filled (5:18) is more easily understood when we go back to the first half which speaks of a fullness of love (3:14–21). We can be 'being filled' (a more correct translation) with His love as a continuing, daily experience. This is the thrust of Paul's prayer. What a wonderful reality.

> To have found God and still to pursue
> Him is the soul's paradox of love.
>
> - Tozer -

Here is a helpful summary quote from Steve DeNeff:

[A person is never so healthy as to be immune from infection] .... So it is that we are called to 'perfect holiness out of reverence for God' (2 Corinthians 7:1), and to 'live in order to please God ... more and more' (1 Thessalonians 4:1). In this sense, we are not absolutely perfect anymore than one can be absolutely full of either food or love. We may be very satisfied for the moment, but if we are normal, we will one day want more to eat and more to love.... 'To have found God and still to pursue Him is the soul's paradox of love,' wrote A. W. Tozer....[17]

---

[17] DeNeff, *Whatever Became of Holiness?* 91.

PART 3: **THE WAY**

How to Become All We Are Meant to Be

Part 3 sets forth the steps to be followed if we are to enjoy all that God has for us. This material provided the motivation for the writing of this book, even though some time was needed to be spent laying foundations in the earlier chapters. This part features the 'how to' of maintaining the life He has for us.

Chapter 8

Total commitment—a human temple of the Holy Spirit. The place of obedience is the starting place as we are dealing with the Owner and Ruler of the whole universe. There is a prayer included that I have seen answered in my life over decades. What does a full commitment look like when we face temptations? The nature of change in our lives is rarely like a tornado: it is usually more like a grain of sand in an oyster. Finally, we ask about 'when suffering comes our way', and anticipate Chapter 10 with the control of our minds.

Chapter 9

A Disciplined Routine—a pattern for progress. We will identify the activities which put us in the place where growth can happen. There is wisdom from the Westminster Confession of Faith on the place of Worship. This does not mean pressure or a legalistic ritual but systematising our personal lifestyle to make for liberty. God calls us to develop convictions in specific areas while respecting the freedom for others to have different ones.

Chapter 10

A Guarded Imagination—a renewed mind, thinking 'Christian-ly'. This has both a negative and positive aspect as we release hurts, and instead see ourselves as God sees us. We will identify ways of handling the ongoing nature of life on a fallen planet, namely, that people will hurt us and we will be damaged unless we learn the freedom of forgiveness. There is recent research on the effect that some computer technology has on the human brain, including pornography and the damage it can do.

Chapter 11

Accountability is needed for government (which is why we have elections). At a personal level, we can be supported by friends in a small group. God introduced the idea of a chosen people to sound forth His praises and to *bless* His people. The importance of being part of a small circle for encouragement and learning is consistent with scripture and has been anointed by God repeatedly. It allows us to harness the dynamic of accountability for our healthy Christian development.

Chapter 12

Investing in others implies the biblical idea of 'discovering a destiny', part of which is the biblical call to discipling. This chapter is an encouragement to pursue the deeper life and invest in others as a step of obedience. We do so knowing we too will be blessed by God and be a blessing to our world hastening a spiritual awakening in our lifetime.

My heart's cry to God is that you will be informed and inspired by the insights offered. They come after a lifetime of seeking to become a godly person and to help others move in that direction as well.

Chapter 8

Total Commitment

Complete and utter obedience

In Part 1, we considered *the Life* which we desire, and in Part 2, *the Truth* about a radiant character, which scripture declares to be possible. What, then, is *the Way*? Linked with this is the importance of *continuing* in the abundant life. It is one thing for an aeroplane to attain cruising altitude, but it is equally important to maintain it.

At the outset, we remembered that every dad longs in his best moments, to be a better husband, father and son, plus being a more useful employer or employee. Just as surely, every woman, whether in the home or work place, can echo the motto of Susanna Wesley who said, "Lord, make my life count." Equally, each young person longs to find a worthwhile future for their one-and-only life. A key is total commitment. Jesus spoke of this in His prayer in John 17:18–19: "As you sent Me into the world, I am sending them into the world. And I give myself entirely to you so they also might be entirely yours" (NLT). There is no more complete commitment than the one *He* made, as He went to the cross.

In this part, we will focus on our responsibility, as we outlined in Chapter 2, referring to Romans 6:12–13. Clearly there is a sense in which God meets us at every point, and the whole process flows from His grace, love and mercy. I strongly believe God can be trusted to do His part. The challenge is whether we are accepting *our* responsibility—remember the way we saw repentance as a two-way communication process in Chapter 5? This begins with a transparent honesty which includes not just sorrow for sin, but also a longing to break from the attitudes and behaviours which flowed from our self-centred lifestyle before our conversion.

Beyond that, we need to be growing in understanding of what it means to have every area of our lives fully surrendered to His lordship. When I made my decision as a child to follow the Lord, all I really had to give him (as I saw it), was my past sins and future hopes—whatever they were. As a high schooler, I had an afternoon job putting flyers in letter boxes for a local supermarket, and when I was paid, I had to make a decision about *giving*. Later, I could give Him my *driving*. I prayed a lot before buying my first car and learned to drive it as part of my Christian commitment. Later I could give Him my *friendships,* especially when it came to relationships, and in particular, *marriage*. I am thankful that He has guided me and blessed me greatly through my wonderful wife and sons. The point is that there was an expansion of areas I could yield, and that has continued throughout the years. As each opportunity opened, it was important to keep affirming His right to control that area.

A prayer that I learned many years ago, which I still use in my devotions each day, is based on Luke 11:9. This is how I pray it:

- Ask—I ask You Father for the health, and strength to serve You and never to fail You.
- Seek—I seek from You the money, and things to provide the resources for a creative and fruitful life.
- Knock—Open the door to the right work that will enable me to make my finest contribution to Your kingdom.[1]

I have prayed those prayers with all my heart and I am honestly amazed at the way in which they have been answered in my life. They come from the book, *I Will Lift Up Mine Eyes*, by a Professor of English literature, and athletics coach, Glenn Clark. Under his heading of 'Dreaming Great Dreams', Clark reminds us that God *wants* to give good gifts to His children. If we think we need something, we should ask. Whether we need a house, a car, spouse, a job, an overseas trip, or an opportunity to study at a particular college, whatever we need, whether large or small, we can ask God for it.

Professor Clark says to be as specific as possible and then begin a pruning process. He suggests using Philippians 4:8 to test your request in order to ensure that it is a 'soul's sincere desire'.[2]

[1] Glenn Clark, *I Will Lift Up Mine Eyes* (The Drift, Evesham, Worcs: Arthur James Limited, 1953), 40–41.
[2] Ibid., 64ff.

Here is how I ask the questions. Whatsoever is:

- *True*—Is it true to my nature? Do my natural interests and gifts lie in this area?
- *Honest*—Am I honestly willing to pay the price if God gives me what I request?
- *Just*—Am I praying for something that belongs to another?
- *Pure*—What are my motives? Would I be *using* people to satisfy my selfish desires? Is any commandment of the Bible violated in this request?
- *Lovely*—Would it make the world a better and more beautiful place?
- *Of Good Report*—Would the news of this answer to prayer encourage people?
- *Excellent and worthy of Praise*—Am I so sure my requests pass the test of the scriptures that I can praise God for His providence, even before the answer to the request has arrived in my life?

I can truthfully say He has been faithful in each area, even though there are many, many areas where I wish I had done better. There is also a deeper area of commitment in that we need to be obedient in regard to our attitudes, forgiving past hurts and leaving them in the past. I remember reading a quote where the writer said, 'Our past wounds need to be *destroyed*, not embalmed.' I have come to see that if we bury them alive, they later explode like a land mine, damaging those whom we love. Implementing Paul's command to "bless and curse not" (Romans 12:14) has been hard to obey when the wounds are significant, but I can honestly say it has been the way of freedom, over and over again.

Salvationist Milton Agnew pictures God's faithfulness in

> ... a simple legend of a poor boy, the son of a widow, who had gathered from the woods a dish of strawberries. As he was returning home with his delicacy, a crusty old man saw his delectable treasure and startled him by calling out: "My lad, let me have your full dish and you take my empty one." Pity for the old man's weakness and helplessness overcame the boy's reluctance to part with his berries. He made the exchange and then went back to the tedious task of again filling the empty dish. Having accomplished this, he returned with it to his mother, to whom he told the story of his adventure. She

examined the vessel, then exclaimed: "Ah, happy are we, my child. The dish is pure gold."[3]

Temptation and the way to freedom in our world

Concerning the nature of our commitment, when it comes to life's temptations—is it complete? Paul instructs us, "Do not let sin reign in your mortal body...." (Romans 6:12). As we discovered in Chapter 4, that implies it is something *we* are to do. The command 'do not let' shows our responsibility to do our part. He also instructs the Colossians to "put to death whatever belongs to your earthly nature" (3:5).

Peter writes that we are to make every effort to be found spotless, blameless and at peace with Him, (2 Peter 3:14), and James instructs: "Resist the devil and he will flee from you" (James 4:7). These are all part of a larger whole because every New Testament command is something we are to do.

> Peter writes that we are to make every effort to be found spotless, blameless and at peace with Him

One reason why we fail in the struggle with temptation is that we have misunderstood living by faith to mean that we are to stop striving, sit back and let the Spirit do the work. To identify our part as being 'in the energy of the flesh' is to ignore our responsibility in the process.

Bishop J. C. Ryle asks:

Is it wise to proclaim in so bald, naked, and unqualified a way as many do, that the holiness of converted people is by faith only, and not at all by personal exertion? Is it according to the proportion of God's Word? I doubt it. That faith in Christ is the root of all holiness ... no well-instructed Christian will ever think of denying. But surely the Scriptures teach us that in

---

[3] Milton S. Agnew, *Transformed Christians—New Testament Messages on Holy Living* (Kansas City, MO: Beacon Hill Press of Kansas City, 1974), 22.

following holiness the true Christian needs personal exertion and work as well as faith.[4]

Paul picks up the partnership between us and the Holy Spirit when he writes: "... work out your own salvation ... for it is God who works in you both to will and to do for His good pleasure" (Philippians 2:12–13). The New Living Translation helpfully translates it "... put into action God's saving work in your lives, obeying God with deep reverence and fear. For God is working in you, giving you the desire to obey him and the power to do what pleases him."

> One reason why we fail in the struggle with temptation is that we have misunderstood living by faith to mean that we are to stop striving, sit back and let the Spirit do the work.

I am reminded of a missionary who was approached one day by a converted cannibal chief, asking if he could have a brief vacation from being a Christian—just for a few hours, so he could go and kill a certain neighbouring chief who had been a long-term rival. He assured the missionary that he would be right back to continue his Christian life. It relates to who the believer now is, and Who God is. It is not so far removed from our Western world, where a man at the Bible study shared freely his struggle with pornography, and how desperate he was to be free. Later, when the leader quietly offered to fit a filter to the computer, he said "Not yet".

This is where the word 'repentance' carries its full meaning: 'Sorry enough to quit'.

Sadly, we are sorry only for the consequences of our sins. They created problems we could never have foreseen, but many of us would try again if we thought we would not get caught next time, and that things would turn out differently. As we have noted in Chapter 5, repentance is like doing a 'U-turn'. It is a change of direction—a complete reorientation of our life to please God, not ourselves. It is the reprogramming of our minds to which Paul urges us in

---

[4] Quoted by Bridges, *The Pursuit of Holiness*, 21.

Philippians 2:5: "Let this mind be in you which was also in Christ Jesus."

This goes beyond turning over a new leaf. We have probably turned over more leaves than those to be found in the nearby park in winter time. When David asked God to create in him a clean heart (Psalm 51:10), he was asking for more than having his sin-stained heart washed. He wanted a change that went much deeper. The changes are not like a tornado. They are more like a grain of sand in an oyster. As David Seamands correctly says: "The aim of God in self-surrender is not the destruction of self; it is the birth and the growth of the true self He intended you to be."[5] True freedom is not in the absence of slavery but in the presence of a wonderful Master.

There is a wonderful story of the famous missionary, E. Stanley Jones, who recognised this need in his life, so he went to the chapel alone with pen and paper and carefully made a list of all he felt he could usefully contribute to God's kingdom. He then prayerfully placed it on the altar. After a time of waiting on God, he sensed something was not quite right, so he removed the list, and then placed a blank piece of paper on the altar with only his signature at the bottom. That made the difference.

When Leonardo da Vinci had completed painting *The Last Supper*, a visiting friend commented on the cups: "What delicate colour and so perfectly portrayed." The master exclaimed, "I don't want you to see the cups; I want you to see the Christ!" He painted them out, and there are now no cups on the table in the masterpiece.

The priority of persistence

The Bible has many examples of persistence in the face of trials. Consider Noah, Abraham, Jacob, Joseph, Moses, Joshua, Hannah, Samuel, Deborah, the Prophets, Esther, and in the New Testament the Twelve disciples, Stephen, Paul, to name just some. Their commitment was total—at least by the end of their lives. The truth is that we will face temptations throughout our journey. Joshua had struggles throughout the conquest of Canaan, as did other leaders in the Old Testament. The best illustration, however, is the Lord, from beginning to end, but especially in Gethsemane, when He was

---

[5] David A. Seamands, *Putting Away Childish Things* (Wheaton, IL: Victor Books, 1982), 130.

tempted to escape and clearly (and understandably) wanted to avoid the cross. Then on the cross when taunted, He could have called legions of angels but in so doing would have failed to achieve His Father's will (Matthew 26:53).

I have watched wind surfers who were just starting, and they seemed to fall almost every couple of minutes (a bit like toddlers learning to walk), but it is not worth comparing with the delight when they get the knack. It is the persisting that develops character and self-discipline.

As Oswald Chambers so wisely said,

God can give us pure hearts in an instant, but He cannot quickly give us Christian character. That takes time and can come only through a series of right moral choices. Temptation is the proving ground of those choices and no one is exempt, not even our Lord Himself.[6]

Each time we choose the difficult, but right option, we grow. Chambers quoted the 1930's Broadway play and movie script, *Green Pastures*, when in a moment of acceptance and surrender one character says "Lord, I ain't much, but I's all I's got!"[7]

That is quite profound because it is what the Lord is looking for. This is why Peter urges Christians to "make every effort to apply the benefits of these promises to your life. Then your faith will produce a life of moral excellence. A life of moral excellence leads to knowing God better. Knowing God leads to self-control. Self-control leads to patient endurance, and patient endurance leads to godliness" (2 Peter 1:5–6 NLT).

It is this discovery that is a surprise to many new Christians. When the euphoria of conversion and the wonder of release from guilt before a holy God has settled, we come face to face with the reality of the need to grow in holiness by daily obedience. Solomon's prayer at the dedication of the temple reflects a total commitment (1 Kings 8:56–62). However, sadly, it had faded by the end of his life (1 Kings 11:1–8), which tells the tragic tale of his gradual loss of faith in the Lord as the one and only God. This resulted in terrible consequences for himself and the nation, not to mention the children

---

[6] Quoted by Seamands, *Putting Away Childish Things*, 94–95.
[7] Ibid., 103.

he burned alive when worshipping Molech, in direct disobedience to the Lord (Leviticus 18:21, Deuteronomy 17:16–17).

It is here that the knowledge of scripture is so vital. The pilot who has to fly using his instruments learns that he cannot operate depending on feelings or intuition. Too often, these are misleading, and the consequences really do matter.

My adult years have included four years of school teaching, both primary then secondary. During that latter time, I began to lead and speak at high school camps and youth meetings. Teenagers have a special place in my heart. As I look back at comments young people have made, I am amazed at the profound effect those school years have had on us all, myself included. As far as I can see most, if not all of us, have had painful times in the class room and playground— unkind remarks, or when we failed a test, broke a school rule, or were bullied. The later years have also meant disappointments, whether in the home, scouts, sporting club, or market place. Sadly, the scars often remain into adulthood. One might well ask if the damage can ever be undone. The following is encouraging in this regard:

I heard a beautiful testimony from one of the converts in a Bill Glass Prison Crusade.... They told us he was known as one of the tough guys of the prison. He accepted Christ as his Saviour on the first night of the crusade. A few days later he said, 'You know, something's happening to me. I don't really understand it and I sure can't explain it. I got up this morning and I didn't scream and holler like I usually do. Even my cellmates commented about it. The only way I can describe it is it's like someone took the old tape which had been playing in my mind since I was a kid, and put a new tape in and it's playing new talk and new music'.

.... When an airplane crashes, a lot of attention is focused on the 'little black box'. This is the crashproof, fireproof, waterproof steel box which contains the recording of everything the pilots said and did just prior to the accident. When the investigators get that then they are able to make an accurate determination of who or what was at fault.

In a sense God has built into every one of us a device similar to the flight recorder. Our memories contain the unerring and inerasable record of our every word and action. Conscience is a part of this—so many of us constantly struggle with a sense of unresolved guilt. Sometimes it is a mixture of real guilt and childish pseudo guilt. In any case, we are like the psalmist who said, 'My sin is ever before me.' Note he did not say 'was'. He put it in the present tense. We say the trouble is our past, but the real trouble is that the past is not in the past. It is in the present and we wear it around our necks like a chain.[8]

Fenelon spoke of the 'crucifixion of the will' but this is not its obliteration. Resurrection follows for the Christian, because God is not destroying us but transforming us, so that we increasingly will what God wills. Glenn Clark urges us to pray "I will to will the WILL of God."[9]

Little children often fear the dark when it comes time to turn off the lights at night. Then parents hear about the 'bogeyman'. They usually try showing that there is no bogeyman under the bed, but it usually doesn't work. "They come out at dark", says the child. The best response is to be with the child as they go to sleep, confident that the loving parent will protect them. There is a similar dynamic with Christians who are fearful of what God will do if we trust Him to guide our steps. The answer is to strengthen our concept of God and confidence in Him and cultivate an awareness that He can be trusted. He does not deny that fearful times will come but assures us He will be with us when they do.

Permit me to sound a warning about the danger of continuing to allow sins of bitterness and resentment to remain in our heart, as they are a pathway for demons to enter and short-circuit God's work in us. Yes, there is sufficient evidence that Christians can be oppressed and hindered in their service for God by demons. We must be careful not to make ourselves vulnerable in this way.

The early governors of the Australian colony wanted the chaplains to make the convicts 'good', but not to preach too much 'religion'. They failed to understand that in the letter to the Romans, Paul spends the first eight chapters laying a foundation, before addressing the issues of behaviour. The fact is that you cannot have morality without roots. The plant is sustained by its roots and Christians are sustained by their rooted values. Similarly, our individual sins are rooted in the self which is not yet surrendered.

---

[8] Ibid., 136–137.
[9] Clark, *I will lift up Mine Eyes*, 37.

This is the sin *principle* referred to in older translations of Romans 7, as the 'old man'.

This process of shrinking the self until it is out of sight when we honestly face our faults is liberating. To let go deeply inside means our true self is in fact more fulfilled. The fear can be a protective device of the ego to keep the true self from emerging and becoming victorious. But until that false ego dies, the true self cannot emerge. When the true self emerges, the result is that we really begin to live. Seamands comments that "Self-surrender is the ultimate crisis because it is the answer to life. This self dies in order to truly live. This captive self surrenders not to be destroyed, annihilated, or absorbed, but to be liberated to be its true and best self."[10]

> When the true self emerges, the result is
> that we really begin to live.

Milton Agnew picks up the point that our self-surrender does not lead to a vacuum, but rather to something far better.

> The story is told in the *Odyssey* of the alluring sirens who sang so beautifully on the shore rocks that the sailors would steer the ship in their direction and be shipwrecked. Captains of the vessels tried in vain to turn them from their purpose. One put cotton in the sailors' ears to keep out the sound. Another lashed them to the mast. But many ships continued to be lost. Ulysses, however, solved the problem by securing the services of Orpheus, who *presented better, more alluring music* [11] than the sirens. The sailors lost their interest in the sirens.... So it is, that, when allowed to rule, the higher law of the Spirit utterly defeats the lower law of sin and death.[12]

The mention of music raises another part of how we "worship the Lord in the beauty of holiness" (Psalm 29:2). A frequently overlooked factor is the place of the songs we sing and allow to run through our minds during the day. This especially affects our youth with their love of music. Yet many of the secular songs of our day are carrying a tragic message. Contrast that with the way we can have

---

[10] Seamands, *Putting Away Childish Things*, 131.
[11] Italics mine.
[12] Agnew, *Transformed Christians*, 108.

songs from Sunday worship running through our brains, whether driving, mowing, washing dishes, or just weeding the garden. Many are prayers we can be echoing.

We must face the fact that our multicultural society sees *mild* commitment as the best way—always. Steve DeNeff puts it this way: "The dominant virtue in most homes and most churches is moderation. There will always be tremendous pressure placed upon the disciple … toward the more moderate sympathies of a *follower.*"[13]

> Our multicultural society sees *mild* commitment as the best way—always.

When suffering comes

The other place where the nature of our commitment surfaces is in the way we respond to suffering. Christianity is unique in how it handles and transforms our pain. Isaiah 48:10 speaks of being refined "in the furnace of suffering" (NLT), and the Servant of Chapter 53 suffers in order to rescue others. In Romans 5:3-4 Paul affirms that we also "glory in tribulations", knowing that they "produce perseverance, and perseverance character; and character hope" (Romans 5:3-4). James 1:2-4 and other scriptures portray it, not as an inconvenience to be tolerated while standing in line for heaven, but as a means of being conformed into Christ's image (Romans 8:29), becoming like Him in His death (Philippians 3:10). John Stott spoke of our having what he called 'lingering immaturities'[14] and it seems that suffering is part of how the Lord corrects them, and matures our faith.

There is no shortcut. Part of learning obedience means discovering that we were never created for independent action, or being 'self-made'. Rather, God's will is for submission, to love and obey and find that it becomes true for us by the Spirit of obedience. Joseph learned what we all must learn, that God's will was unfolding in all his circumstances, even when he suffered unjustly. His enemies

---

[13] Steve DeNeff, *More Than Forgiveness* (Indianapolis, IN: Wesleyan Publishing House, 2002), 79.

[14] John Stott, *The Radical Disciple—Wholehearted Christian Living* (Nottingham: Inter-Varsity Press, 2010), 46.

were contributing to God's plan for him. I am so amazed to see how, as Norman Grubb said,

> He led his brethren to true repentance and acknowledgement of their sin, which he freely forgave and never withdrew, neither during their father's lifetime, nor after.... [His] self was no longer itself, but the dwelling place of God."[15]

> Joseph learned what we all must learn, that God's will was unfolding in all his circumstances, even when he suffered unjustly.

A different approach

The letter to the Thessalonians was probably one of the first that Paul wrote. We often quote the famous reference in 1 Thessalonians 5:18: "In everything give thanks". Sadly, we often only quote it to others. Later he wrote Ephesians, in which we discover that he has learned a few more things about the Christian life. In Ephesians 5:20 he instructs us to be "giving thanks always *for all* things". He has seen the good that God brought out of apparent disasters in his missionary journeys and now expands the application of the principle.

I learned it in my first parish in Queensland when we studied the series from Bill Bright's Lay Institute for Evangelism *Transferable Concept 4*. He tells the story of a couple travelling home after their engagement party. The woman was driving the car, when an oncoming vehicle forced them off the road into a telephone pole and her fiancé was killed. The result was that, with a burden of grief and false guilt, she had not had quality sleep since. Having been to doctors, psychiatrists, psychologists, ministers, and many others, looking for help, she now feared for her sanity. Bright goes on to say:

> I asked her if she were a Christian, and she said, "Yes." We read Romans 8:28 and I asked, "Do you believe that all things work for good?" She said, "Yes, I believe that." We turned to 1 Thessalonians 5:18. She read it aloud: "In all things give

---

[15] Norman Grubb, *The Liberating Secret* (London: Lutterworth Press, 1964), 56. (Grubb has profound comments in this area, 52–56.)

thanks, for this is the will of God in Christ Jesus concerning you." I said to her, "Have you thanked God for the loss of your loved one?" She was shocked and could hardly believe that she heard me correctly. She looked at me in disbelief as she said, "How can I ever thank God for such a tragic loss?"[16]

He went on to point out that it is really an issue of *trust*, and was able to lead her to pray a prayer of thanks. She returned the next day "literally bubbling over with joy. She said, 'Last night I slept without medication for the first time since the accident.'"[17]

I have made this 'saying thank you in advance' part of my life in response to every annoyance or trouble. I am absolutely convinced that our God is big, and powerful enough, to bring blessing out of *any* and *every* seeming setback, large or small. Part of the holy life is to make this 'faith response' our normal way of responding to the trials which, we are informed, *will* come our way. It is bringing faith to bear and affirming the sovereignty of God as we believe for a blessing we have not yet seen.

> I am absolutely convinced that our God is big, and powerful enough, to bring blessing out of *any* and *every* seeming setback, large or small.

It works—whether it is pain, disappointment or even dealing with the anger that such times generate. It is always "Thank you Lord. You will bring good out of this."

This brings us to the next chapter: A Disciplined Routine—putting ourselves in the place where growth can happen.

[16] Bill Bright, *How to Walk in the Spirit—Transferable Concept 4* (Campus Crusade for Christ, Inc., 1971), 44.
[17] Ibid., 43–45.

A RADIANT CHARACTER

Chapter 9

A Disciplined Routine

The airbus A320 had been in the air just 2 minutes when it encountered a flock of Canadian geese which crippled both engines. This placed at risk all the passengers and the people in the city below.

With just three minutes left in the air, Captain Chesley Sullenberger had no time to read the manual.

In those 180 seconds, he had to:

- Decide where *not* to land—neither the houses, nor the freeway were options.
- Set the aircraft to glide because he now had no engine power.
- Get the nose down to maintain speed.
- Seal all the vents and valves.
- Take a hard turn left to go *with* the river.
- Hit the water, level and nose up.

That was the day when he and many others benefited from his good preparation, training and self-discipline. The truth is that this whole scenario began a long time before, with his upbringing, the decision to become a pilot, his years of training, and the years of experience.[1] He had developed character.

The opportunity does not make the champion or the criminal. It shows him what he has already become in the multitude of little decisions in his everyday life. "Widespread transformation of character through wisely disciplined discipleship to Christ can transform our world. It can disarm the structural evils that have

---

[1] Tom Wright recounts this event in more detail as a very helpful illustration of "character" as he described it earlier in the book. Tom Wright, *Virtue Reborn* (London: SPCK, 2010), 7–8.

always dominated humankind and now threaten to destroy the world."[2]

Being where growth can happen

We can come to a point of heart purity in a moment, as we consecrate ourselves and make a total commitment. However, it takes time to come to a level of maturity in our faith as we remain faithful in the journey, rising above the challenges and set-backs. The tradesman adds experience to his skills with the tools, to become a master builder. Similarly, Christians acquire a stability and radiance of character as they faithfully pursue the goal of the upward call of God in Christ (Philippians 3:14). This is the path to maturity[3] which is much more than simply purity.

> Christians acquire a stability and radiance of character as they faithfully pursue the goal of the upward call of God in Christ (Philippians 3:14).

A farmer is helpless to grow grain; all he can do is to provide the right conditions for the growing of grain. He puts the seed in the ground where the natural forces take over and up comes the grain. That is the way with the Spiritual Disciplines—they are a way of sowing to the Spirit. The Disciplines are God's way of getting us into the ground; they put us where He can work within us and transform us. By themselves the Spiritual Disciplines can do nothing; they can only get us to the place where something can be done. They are God's means of grace. The inner righteousness we seek is not something that is poured on our heads. God has ordained the Disciplines of the spiritual life as the means by which we are placed where He can bless us.[4]

---

[2] Dallas Willard, *The Spirit of the Disciplines* (San Francisco: Harper and Row, 1988), xi. Quoted by Bill Hull, *Choose the Life—Exploring a Faith that Embraces Discipleship* (Grand Rapids, MI: Baker Books, 2004), 61.

[3] A jug and a cup may both be full but one holds more than the other.

[4] Richard J. Foster, *Celebration of Discipline—The Path to Spiritual Growth* (London: Hodder and Stoughton, 1980), 6.

One of the reasons why you are still reading this book is hopefully, to experience an intensifying of your Christian faith. Previous chapters have reminded us that we cannot do it on our own, just as the farmer cannot grow grain without God's help. We have also discovered that he can, and *is* expected to do something. He can provide the right conditions for growth, such as placing the seed in the soil and nourishing the plant as it grows.

Similarly, we can take steps to cultivate holiness by exercising self-discipline and developing holy habits. Richard Foster illustrates this well:

> Picture a narrow ledge with a sheer drop-off on either side. The chasm to the right is the way of moral bankruptcy through human strivings for righteousness. Historically this has been called the heresy of moralism. The chasm to the left is the way of moral bankruptcy through the absence of human strivings. This has been called the heresy of antinomianism. On the ledge there is a path, the Disciplines of the spiritual life. This path leads to the inner transformation and healing for which we seek. We must never veer off to the right or the left, but stay on the path. The path is fraught with severe difficulties, but also with incredible joys. As we travel on this path, the blessing of God will come upon us and reconstruct us into the image of His Son Jesus Christ. We must always remember that the path does not produce the change; it only puts us in the place where the change can occur. This is the way of disciplined grace.[5]

As we tread this path, God will never treat us as robots. Before we became Christians, we had a choice to stay as rebels, or submit to Christ as Saviour and Lord. Now that we have committed our lives to Him, we still have a free will, and God wants us to use it. The very process of making right choices will refine our character and make us champions. There are dynamics that go with living for Him in this fallen world and we must understand them, and harness them.

> God will never treat us as robots.

---

[5] Ibid., 7.

As I reflect on my own journey, and that of those whose lives I have sought to encourage, I am impressed by the fact that the making of the total commitment has not been the hardest part. I can remember messages where the Holy Spirit moved, and I was stirred to say 'yes' to God. Often there was a song to allow me to sing my response and that was welcome too. The hard part came in the following days and weeks, as I sought to put that commitment into practice. Discipleship, I discovered, is more than a program; it is a pursuit.

Studying Scripture

The long history of the church shows that the Bible has been an essential ingredient in having a radiant character, both studied systematically, and also memorized. I find the New King James Version (NKJV) works well for me as much of my early memorizing was in that style of language, but publicly, I usually read from the New Living Translation (NLT). Hence, I use the NKJV for devotions, thus informally revising important memorized verses and then refer when necessary to more contemporary speech. The psalmist said, "Your word I have hidden in my heart, that I might not sin against You" (Psalm 119:11).

When struggling as a young Christian, I attended a convention, and sought counsel. I was grateful for a listening ear, but I wish someone had touched on this principle as well as some of the other ideas we are considering in this last part of the book. DeNeff notes that "Like a good, steady downpour of rain, the Scripture will not create the holes in the roof, but it will surely find them."[6] He also notes that "our minds will never be more holy than our knowledge of Scripture will allow."[7] Such study further strengthens us to hand over our will to the Holy Spirit, and to follow through the disciplines which consolidate our commitment. This allows God's wonderful plan for our lives to unfold.

Christianity is a revealed faith. The written Word of God is vital in fine-tuning my understanding of God. Personal devotional reading of scripture and books which are consistent with it, are foundational. A close Salvationist friend said William Booth urged his men to read five chapters a day. I have also found this model helpful especially in

[6] DeNeff, *Whatever Became of Holiness?* 118.
[7] Ibid., 115.

more recent years. However, sometimes I read much less to allow my mind to focus on significant passages.

Participation in a mid-week Home Bible Study fellowship has enhanced the learning as well, and in my case, the opportunity to attend a college, and later do systematic study by distance education, added yet more understanding of God. The sermon on Sunday does not need to be all new material to be useful. I do not so much need to be *told*, as to be *reminded,* so the process is still precious, plus I get to greet my friends who love me and I love them.

I am reminded that a commitment to God is a relationship just like a marriage, and our regular, submissive reading of the Bible is part of the communication component. He speaks through 'the sacred page'. It has been said that 'many want a wedding day, but not all want a marriage'. It is the day-by-day sharing of the journey that is the challenge and the real source of joy. The experience of a happy Christian marriage is an advanced sampling of what heaven will be like. To be loved and accepted and to share the 'ups and downs' that are part of life in a fallen world is truly precious. As well as highs and lows, there is what one hymn writer described as

... All the other days that make my life,
Marked by no special joy or grief or strife,
Days filled with quiet duties, trivial care,
Burdens too small for other hearts to share.[8]

The author then continues in the next verse with, "Spend Thou these days with me ..." We are making a journey with our unseen Friend, with Whom we walk, and talk, and to Whom we listen.

The first thing that God identified as 'not good' was *loneliness* (Genesis 2:18), and it was identified as such before the tragedy of the Fall. It was companionship that Adam needed, and Eve was created to meet that need, and yet we know that this life is to be lived in the light of a deeper reality which Jesus called the 'kingdom of heaven'. It is the sharing of that relationship with our Lord and with His people which is the key to changes for the better.

I do not always find it easy to compare my everyday 'nuts and bolts' responsibilities with the lives of those who have felt called to

---

[8] R. Deck (Hymn Writer), *The Keswick Hymn Book, "I Take Thy promise, Lord"* (London: Marshall, Morgan & Scott, Ltd., n.d.), Hymn 107.

the seclusion of the monastery or retreat centre. Life has its 'rough and tumbles' as well as the demands of people around us, including family, friends and work mates. However, I sometimes wonder whether our preference is to be busy rather than being still, and taking time for devotions. That is why I believe the discipline of a godly routine is such a help.

Keeping a journal

The other resource in this is the practice of journalling[9] which makes our thinking specific. I use the acrostic A.C.T.S.:

- *Adoration*—what can I admire about God in the passage of the Bible I have just read?

- *Confession*—what apologies do I need to make to God and change in things I think about and do?

- *Thanksgiving*—what gratitude do I need to express? God has been so good to me.

- *Supplication*—prayers for others, including leaders, missionaries and my family.

Asking these and reflecting on the answer, has greatly helped in my own journey, along with many Christians, because it has given devotions a framework.[10]

> I sometimes wonder whether our preference is to be busy rather than being still, and taking time for devotions.

The importance of worship

When I was seeking to define 'disciple' as part of my ministry, as well as in my own journey, I recognised that truth about God should lead to an obedient life. Initially, I was not sure what to call it, but then realised that it is part of worship, which we too often think of as just what happens in church. Of course, worship is a major purpose

---

[9] William Backus, *Finding the Freedom of Self-Control* (Minneapolis, MN: Bethany House Publishers, 1987), 154–156 has an excellent section on how use journaling to help break a bad habit.

[10] Gordon MacDonald's book *Ordering Your Private World* (Chicago: Moody Press, 1984), 140–147, also includes valuable insights on this.

for Christians to come together on the Lord's day, but in fact all of life is intended by our Creator to be lived in obedience to His wise counsel. This is worship as well.

The *Westminster Confession* correctly says that our chief end is to "glorify God, and to enjoy Him forever".[11] Because He loves us and wants the best for us, God has some specific designs and desires for human beings, as the apex of His creation. Thus, holiness is not a suggestion or an option, but a command, and *all* our expressions of obedience are worship, even though they do not carry the formal 'tag' usually linked with a church service.

One of my most significant discoveries in this area came when I learned to thank God for the good that He promises to bring out of every experience, as we noted in the last chapter (Romans 8:28). That means that when I get a flat tyre, because all things are working for my good, if I love God and am called according to His purpose, I can start saying 'thanks' in anticipation of the good coming from that particular event. I now realise that this also, is an act of worship which does not depend on my feelings but is an act of my will stirring me to remember His sovereignty over every part of my life. Thus, each small trial is in fact working in me a definite benefit. As both Paul in Romans 5:3–5 and James in 1:2–4 remind us, 'troubles teach patience'.

When my hand performs a difficult manoeuvre, I can admire the Creator and say, "well done" to Him for the design so evident in my body, and when I see breathtaking scenery, or the flash of a bolt of lightning, I can affirm my response— "Lord I am impressed." The delight of little children or the kindness of a friend all can evoke a 'yay God' moment.

In other words, every moment of every day, I am living in touch with my Lord via the Holy Spirit. Clearly this goes beyond just what happens at the weekly church service, though that sets the stage for the events of the week. It is even better if I am able to be at two services. So, I do not decide on Sunday morning whether or not I am going to church. That is part of my routine. When I wake each day, sometimes feeling somewhat weary and 'whacked', I do not decide

---

[11] "Shorter Catechism, Q.1.", of the Westminster Confession, http://www.reformed.org/documents/wsc/index.html?_top=http://www.reformed.org/documents/WSC.html.

whether to meet the Lord in Quiet Time; that is part of my routine. It is a divine appointment with my best Friend.

I mentioned public church services earlier, and, in the fellowship where I grew up, singing was a part of that. The songs I now let run through the corridors of my brain during life's boring routine tasks, fit here too. Whether gardening or driving I can reflect on songs I have memorized from singing them, often with God's people, and the prayers in the songs become a private anthem. One evening a group of us Queenslanders decided to rent a car and drive home from Melbourne straight through to Brisbane—1600 kilometres. (There was an airline strike at the time.) My turn to drive came at two o'clock in the morning. I said to the passengers, "I'm going to sing out loud. That way you'll know I'm awake and it will help me stay awake." I was able to sing for two hours with the only repetition being the choruses of some of the songs. That is part of worship too, and I believe it really helps.

Unfortunately, some contemporary church music seems to be 'all about me' and I do not find those as helpful. But there are plenty of excellent contemporary songs, as well as the majestic ones from our Christian heritage. That has been one of the rediscoveries of the last fifty years. Believers have been helped to focus on God as they have sung *to* Him. The danger lies when the lyrics are so vague that they could be sung to Krishna or Buddha, as easily as to the God of the Bible.

Will Sangster wrote a book called *The Pure in Heart,* and the 'how to' part contains a chapter entitled 'The Way is Worship'. He studied the saints of various traditions and discovered the common ground in this area, namely, the blend of adoration—gazing on God as revealed in Jesus, plus faithful obedience to His every wish. It means looking, loving, and longing to be more like Him. Paul described it in 2 Corinthians 3:18 with the idea that as we look at a picture of the Master it becomes increasingly a mirror reflecting His likeness. "... as the Spirit of the Lord works within us, we become more and more like Him and reflect His glory even more" (NLT). Speaking of the saints, Sangster adds:

> They are certain that God is on the throne of the universe. All things are in His loving hands. He permits things to happen which we humans call disasters but—because it is *His* universe and no other's—He does not even *permit* anything to

happen out of which He cannot bring good. To every event, therefore, the saint says with the Divine Son: 'Even so, Father, for so it seemed good in Thy sight.'[12]

Naturally, the enemy of our souls will do everything to disrupt such a wonderful interaction between the believer and the Lord. One of his prime strategies is busyness, and in a world of mobiles (cell phones), emails and text messages, there is a sense in which we are always 'on call'. Please be brave enough to turn off any distractive devices when in church, or having private devotions, or at very least, on 'silent', if it must be active. One benefit of devotions in the midnight hours is that it is not always the appropriate time to make a phone call. If you want to get maximum efficiency out of study, have it off then too. The sound of a signal coming in does make us 'lose our thread', and there is a slight stimulus of the thought that there is a message for '*me*'.[13]

Another way we can be distracted is to let our minds wander, such as to dwell on the unkindnesses of others, whether done to ourselves or someone else we care about. "How could they be so mean?" we ask. Then we dwell on what we would say if given half a chance. We begin to put together scenarios of "what we'll say, if they say...." The following sample scriptures are very relevant:

- "Whatever things are true, ... noble, ... just, ... pure, ... lovely, ... of good report, if there is any virtue and if there is anything praiseworthy—meditate on these things" (Philippians 4:8).

- "Be anxious for nothing, but in everything by prayer and supplication, with thanksgiving, let your requests be made known to God; and the peace of God, which surpasses all understanding, will guard your hearts and minds through Christ Jesus" (Philippians 4:6–7).

- "Bless those who persecute you; bless and do not curse" (Romans 12:14). I have proven that whenever the evil one attacks my thoughts, *blessing* the aggressor helps to change things, and protects my mind from the distraction. It is totally counter-culture, but it is biblical and it does work.

- [We are to bring] every thought into captivity to the obedience of Christ ... (2 Corinthians 10:5).

---

[12] W. E. Sangster, *The Pure in Heart* (London: The Epworth Press, 1954), 204.
[13] For further comment on this see the next chapter—A Guarded Imagination.

- Jesus said, "Don't worry about tomorrow...." (Matthew 6:34 NLT).

It is normal to have a concern for our future, whether it is a possible loss of job, home, loved one or even the political arena as laws are proposed that will undermine our freedoms. Our Lord's wise counsel is to live one day at a time.

Another reason why we struggle to be holy is that we have not developed a hatred of sin. We need to ask the Lord to show us just how serious the problem is. Take, for example, those times when *we* are displeased with our sin. God shows us an area of weakness, 'evil speaking' for instance. We determine in our Quiet Time not to criticize another at all that day. Before lunch we have several conversations, and in one we fail in our resolution—the very one for which we asked God's help! When we stop for lunch we are frustrated and discouraged at our dismal performance. But is our pain primarily that we hate the sin of gossip, or is it that we are faced with our inability to control our behaviour? Is the point of pain, a broken heart for saddening God again, or is it a wounded personal pride that hates such reminders of our own weakness? Remember the comments about pride in Chapter 5 and the reminder that the Lord can take us forward.

> Our Lord's wise counsel is to live
> one day at a time.

Pharaoh and Balaam, Saul and Judas all said, "I have sinned", but none showed a hatred of sin, or a desire for holiness. David's prayer in Psalm 51:10–12 stands in marked contrast when he prays for a clean heart and a restoration of the joy of his salvation. This highlights a vital issue which Bridges faces squarely:

> It is time for us Christians to face up to our responsibility for holiness. Too often we say we are 'defeated' by this or that sin. No, we are not defeated; we are simply disobedient! It might be well if we stopped using the terms 'victory' and 'defeat' to describe our progress in holiness. Rather we should use the terms 'obedience' and 'disobedience'. When I say I am

defeated by some sin, I am unconsciously slipping out from under my responsibility.[14]

In a nutshell, we are called to live in the presence of God with a conscious effort to guard our minds and let every thought be in captivity to Jesus as Lord. Remember 2 Corinthians 10:5.

Brother Lawrence, a famous monk, was recognised for the phrase "practising the presence of God". It did not matter whether he was doing his kitchen duties or his devotional exercises, he did so with an awareness that it was all for the Lord.

Convictions in specific areas

Paul urges the Christians in Rome to develop their own convictions while allowing others the freedom to differ with them (Romans 14:4). It is a wonderful passage providing for freedom in Christ, as well as integrity and strength of character. Sadly today, it is generally frowned upon for *Christians* to have conviction, (that is labelled 'legalism' or 'intolerance'), but it seems to be OK for cult groups and political groups such as environmentalists and Marxists to have non-negotiable convictions. Some Christians even feel they must apologize for their views, 'lest they give offence'.

God's Word, however, identifies areas where we should think through our position, in a way that can be defended from the Bible, on such issues as: permissible foods, alcohol and drugs, observance of holy days. A father who is an occasional drinker is seen as inconsistent when he tells a teenage son to fully abstain from drugs. Additional areas where Christians need to develop convictions in the 21st century include: television, DVDs, Internet games, movies, Facebook, abortion, euthanasia, drugs (including tobacco), quasi-religious groups. For example: Freemasons, some hobbies, sport, environmental issues, to name a few.

Helpful questions we can ask ourselves include:

- "Can I ask God's blessing on the thing I am about to do?"
- "Does doing this thing build me up—physically, mentally and spiritually?"
- "Can this thing enslave me if I do it?"
- "Will my doing this thing appear sinful or godless to others?"

---

[14] Bridges, *The Pursuit of Holiness*, 84.

- "If I do this thing, is there a possibility that someone else will be caused to stumble or fall?"
- "Am I in any doubt at all about doing this thing?"
- "Would doing this thing embarrass me if Christ were to come just now?"[15]

An additional three tests are:

- *Secrecy?* Do I need to keep it a secret? Can I tell it? Right is never afraid of light! "Men loved darkness rather than light, because their deeds were evil" (John 3:19). If I have to hide it, cover it up, keep it a secret, there is probably something wrong with it.

- *Universality?* Would I be willing for everybody, every Christian, to do this? Suppose my pastor, our deacons, my Sunday school teacher, my parents, my best friends did this, would I respect them? If it would not be OK for every other Christian, how can it be all right for me?

- *Prayer?* Can I honestly ask the Lord to bless me in the doing of this? I should not engage in any activity which I cannot honestly ask God to bless.

Our convictions will degenerate into resolutions and then fade altogether unless we make a quality commitment to live by them. This means we do much more than go forward at a meeting if there is a call for public commitment, or sign a card, or even have a genuine experience of the Holy Spirit's cleansing work. It requires a level of desperation to allow our decision to follow Christ to flow on to our everyday ethics. We do not just say "our future is God's"; we live by our convictions for Him as the future unfolds day by day.

> Our convictions will degenerate into resolutions and then fade altogether unless we make a quality commitment to live by them.

Too often Satan deludes us with the 'just one more time' line until our resolve disintegrates. Sadly, we find ourselves going on as

---

[15] Don Hardgrave, *You Can Know God's Will* (Macgregor, Qld: A Pleasant Surprise Ltd., 1990), 20.

before, except that we are even more pessimistic, closer to cynicism and harder for the Holy Spirit to reach next time. Key insight: 'Never let an exception occur'. Whether it is that food with lots of sugar we should avoid, the television program we should switch off, or the friend we should stop seeing, every time we say 'yes' to temptation, we make it harder to say 'no' the next time.

The painful truth is that we have developed 'habit patterns' of sin. These may include shading the facts a little bit when it suits us or browsing magazines that do not edify. But the habits will never be changed until we make a basic commitment to a life of holiness without exceptions.

Too often we treat sin too lightly saying, "it doesn't matter", but it does. Every time we place our will ahead of God's will, and only sin 'a little', we are delaying our progress in transformation. Bridges asks:

> Can you imagine a soldier going into battle with the aim of "not getting hit very much"? The very suggestion is ridiculous. His aim is not to get hit at all! Yet if we have not made a commitment to holiness without exception, we are like a soldier going into battle with the aim of not getting hit very much. We can be sure if that is our aim, we will be hit—not with bullets, but with temptation over and over again.[16]

> Too often Satan deludes us with the 'just one more time' line until our resolve disintegrates.

Another way that we can recognise our changed attitude comes at those times when we do fall. Previously we would whisper, "Sorry, God," and hurry on. Now, we are determined to identify the trap and avoid it next time. We ask questions like, "How did I get caught? What steps will I take to prevent it from happening next time? What people and places should I avoid? What magazines shouldn't I read? What thoughts shouldn't I harbour?" We acknowledge that sin draws on desire, so we avoid advertising that could lead us into materialism. If we are inclined toward lust, we therefore refrain from watching inappropriate programs (even many advertisements violate Philippians 4:8), or reading certain material.

---

[16] Bridges, *The Pursuit of Holiness*, 96.

Daniel made up his mind not to defile himself with the king's food (Daniel 1:8). The scripture shows how he graciously followed through on this, but the starting point was a decision that every part of every day was to be lived as unto the Lord.

Gordon MacDonald records[17] how John Sculley, former executive at Pepsi, affirmed the way young up-and-coming executives were encouraged to include physical fitness into their normal day with a gym made available to assist them. While we do not need to go to such lengths in our service for the Lord, it is useful to be reminded that discipline in every facet of life flows on in a benefit to other areas as we develop an ordered mind.

Debt wrecks many a marriage and career, so a conviction that "I should get out of debt as soon as practicable", needs to translate into self-discipline in two areas:

1) A conscious choice to not spend money I do not have. Sometimes we spend to feel good rather than because we need it, and we call it 'retail therapy'.

2) A deliberate choice to get out of debt, beginning with the smallest as a focus, and then the next smallest. The boost of encouragement that comes when that debt is cleared, is enhanced by the extra funds now available to tackle the next smallest. It means a new freedom in our lives.

Another area which has been important to God's people over the years is fasting. It certainly was important when the Jewish people faced possible extermination by the evil Haman, and Queen Esther went in to plead with the king on their behalf (Esther 4:16–17).

Jesus did say *"When* you fast, anoint your head and wash your face...." (Matthew 6:17), and again when asked about this, He made reference to the fasting of his future followers *"when* the bridegroom will be taken away from them" (Matthew 9:15). So, what does this mean to a culture that emphasises getting fit, and books on dieting, but seems reluctant to make the kind of self-sacrifice which the concept entails.

---

[17] MacDonald, *Rebuilding Your Broken World*, 225–226.

> A loving father wants his children to be
> obedient, because it is to *their* advantage.
> So does our heavenly Father.

One area we can all consider is to fast from things such as television which will free up more time as well as protect us from ungodly images and advertising. Some have done this during Lent prior to Easter, for example, and been surprised at the benefit. World and local news is readily available from less time-consuming sources. For those choosing to fast in regard to food, it is advisable to seek appropriate advice. Bill Bright has an excellent resource on fasting in preparation for spiritual awakening. It includes wise counsel about how to start and especially how to end a fast in such a way as not to damage your body.[18] This new approach will take time and self-discipline but it is eminently worthwhile. A loving father wants his children to be obedient, because it is to *their* advantage. So does our heavenly Father.

Hull has a useful reminder about discipline: He points out that:

A lack of strong sustaining vision explains why most high school foreign language classes in the U.S. don't work. They may be required classes, but unless the students have the vision to really learn another language, there is usually very little benefit.[19]

Contrast that with students from the Third World wanting to migrate to a Western country to better themselves, or a man learning German to better communicate with the lady with whom he has fallen in love. If we are seeing the disciplined life as a key to effective service and a wonderful relationship with our risen Lord, it all becomes worthwhile but it is never easy. Usually personal discipline is developed in a context of imposed discipline. This is a timely reminder to us all that when we are placed in a setting where we have to 'do as we are told', it will help if we remember that principle. It applies in the home, classroom and market place. It applies in ministry and sadly, far too many worthy efforts have been sabotaged

---

[18] Bill Bright, *The Coming Revival* (Orlando FL: NewLife publications—Campus Crusade for Christ, 1995), 143–151.

[19] Hull, *Choose the Life*, 90. It is an outstanding resource on discipleship and positively addresses many ideas in this book.

by failure in this area. It begins when we are young but, in reality, continues throughout life.

Hull quotes Bill Thrall and Bruce McNicol who helpfully emphasise that "submission is a love word before it is an authority word ..."[20]

Chapters 2–3 gave us details of outstanding people whose lives God has greatly used. Many had unforgettable experiences when God touched their lives, but we need to remember that no experience, no matter how wonderful, is a substitute for a disciplined, daily walk with God, including a quality time alone with Him and day-by-day obedience to the voice of the Holy Spirit. No apprentice would expect to master a skill unless he spent lots of time with the experienced tradesman, watching, listening and interacting.

> Submission is a love word
> before it is an authority word.
>
> - Hull -

In a secular world where it is easy to think and act as if God does not exist, a disciplined routine is one we all must work on but it is eminently worthwhile, and means that we can take advantage of the next step—a guarded imagination.

---

[20] Ibid., 157.

Chapter 10

A Guarded Imagination

Dr Frederick Banting was working one night studying the literature available on diabetes. It was seriously limited with vague ideas and accounts of experiments with dogs and conflicting theories. He went wearily to bed and woke at two o'clock in the morning with an idea which he wrote down—just a few short sentences, then went back to sleep. Those notes led to the discovery of insulin which has brought relief to thousands, but they came as his subconscious mind had processed the data while he was asleep.

Personally, even though I will have done much preparation previously, I have found that a short time praying and reflecting on a theme or a passage of scripture before retiring for the night, will usually be an invaluable part of the process of preparing a message. I should add that I do not clutter my mind, with electronic data or entertainment. Further, I have sought to be diligent in forgiving past hurts and thus minimizing debris from the past from that part of my thinking.

Here is a useful parable: Imagine a new ruler winning control of a country by a coup. Among the cheering crowd are some who still have a heart for the old king. They will cheer with the rest when a new achievement is announced but deep down they will secretly scheme and look for ways to bring the new guy down. It is a picture of some deeply submerged aspects of our mental makeup. They may not be noticed readily but will want to sabotage our best efforts, bringing reminders of past failures and inadequacies to undermine our efforts to be single-minded in pleasing God. Sometimes it is simply an overactive desire to have a perfect performance echoing demands from past authority figures no longer there. Guarding the mind is essential.

It had been raining heavily so when it stopped, Mark Baxter and his family went for a walk in the park. Suddenly the dog, then his daughter, disappeared! The dog had been splashing in the water and suddenly was gone. Then the three-year-old little girl went too. He immediately realised what had happened. A storm drain had burst its cover and the girl and the dog had been sucked down into the drain itself. The father guessed that the drain would probably go into the nearby river, so he sprinted 100 metres, to the riverbank and there she was floating down-stream in her red raincoat. He rescued her, shocked but thankfully still alive.

Describing his frantic dash afterwards, Mark said, "Every time I thought a bad thought, I forced myself to think of something else."[1] Therein lies the secret. He had figured out in a millisecond what had happened and what to do, but he needed to keep a tight rein on his thoughts. A disciplined mind was vital. However, that way of thinking is not developed overnight. He worked for the Royal Air Force and learned self-discipline as part of his vocation. It is the same principle, whether we are learning to play tennis, drive a car, play an instrument or teach a class.

> Every time I thought a bad thought,
> I forced myself to think of something else.
>
> - Baxter -

Living in an era of great change

My father-in-law was born in 1904. The changes in his lifetime were amazing, with planes and cars revolutionising transport, media changes with the advent of movies, and two world wars re-arranging the super-power hierarchy, just to name a few. However, in my own lifetime the changes have also been amazing, especially in recent decades. We have seen the rise of religion as a factor in conflict (in the mid-20th century 25 percent of wars were related to religion. Since 2000 it is 43 percent).[2] Further, the Christian faith which gave us our present democratic society with its hospitals, education, scientific benefits and so on, has been largely ignored by the media (unless it is to discredit belief, by focussing on the inexcusable, past

---

[1] Tom Wright, *Virtue Reborn* (London: SPCK, 2010), 10. This is called 'thought displacement'.
[2] John Micklethwait and Adrian Wooldridge, *God is Back—How the Global Rise of Faith Is Changing the World* (Great Britain: Allen Lane, 2009), 24.

mistreatment of children by a very small minority). Evolution now has a stranglehold on education in the West, even though it is about the past, and so remains experimentally unprovable because it is not repeatable. Obviously, it is impossible to prove anything scientifically without being able to repeat the experiment.[3] It was introduced into Australian schools in 1962 when I was in Year 11 at High School. It is no surprise to observe from church membership graphs that by 1965, attendance and membership were in decline.[4]

More recent changes include computers, rock music, mobile phones and the internet and these have touched people greatly. The internet has brought ready access to information from around the world and made a way for people to access the gospel in previously closed nations. However, with it has also come the invasion of pornography, which is described by church leaders as 'ruining the church from within'. Do we need to be reminded that lust is a sin? (Consider Job 31:1; Matthew 5:28; 15:10–19 and the New Testament letters.) This has a considerable bearing on our quest for a radiant character, because the imagination of people is involved more than ever before in history.

The subconscious is extremely powerful. It is rather like a computer in our head. When we walk, run, or catch a ball, the coordination is all done subconsciously. Similarly, when driving, the various tasks are performed mainly without our 'thinking about it'. This mechanism makes possible the formation of habits which save so much time and stress when doing life's routine tasks. This function is one reason why, when developing a new habit or breaking an old one, *we don't let an exception occur*—especially in the first three weeks. If we do, the subconscious takes note and softly says, "You don't really mean that resolution or you'd be consistent."

Viktor Frankl was a Jewish psychiatrist trained in the school of determinism which taught that our past and our environment determined our behaviour. He developed what he later called *logo therapy* as he coped with the horrors of the Nazi concentration

---

[3] For more information, see: www.creation.com. There are over 10,000 well researched articles by highly qualified personnel which are both informative and inspirational.

[4] I recognize that the arrival of television, the 'pill', and other changes affected public morality but the evidence of the seriously detrimental influence of the evolutionary theory to Western culture's morality is clear: "If there is no God, what is the basis for right and wrong?"

camps (Auschwitz). While he was being tortured he thought about how he would describe the ordeal to his students when the war was over! He observed that there was a constant environment for *all* the prisoners and noted the way some were crushed and others came through, especially those caring for their fellows. His research demolished much of Freud's assumptions and ideas. The change began one day when he was stark naked and the Gestapo interrogator demanded his wedding ring. He realised that there was one thing they could not take away, his freedom to choose his response. He became famous for the saying, "The last of the human freedoms is to choose one's attitude in any given set of circumstances."[5]

I believe he is right. We are the ones who determine our attitudes in every situation, whether we know it or not. In this unpredictable and changing world, the one thing we can always control is the way we think. While we have very limited control over circumstances or the actions of others, we *can* control our reactions to them. Anyone who will work at it can learn how to think more positively and operate with a better attitude, regardless of circumstances, temperament, or intellect.

> A destiny is something we discover
> rather than invent.

Several decades ago I learned another idea which has served me very well both in times of decision making and also when I have felt rejected, after trying my best. It has been that of having a personal affirmation which is in my journal-note book, and I still review it as part of my devotions. It took time to prepare and, in many ways, a destiny is something we discover rather than invent. It is a bit like Captain Cook, *discovering* rather than *inventing* Australia, or Columbus *finding* the American continent. It was already there in the providence of God. In Appendix C, I have included extracts from mine to get you started, but make it yours, leaving out and adding until you can 'own it'.

---

[5]John C. Maxwell, *Your Attitude—Key to Success* (San Bernardino, CA: Here's Life Publishers Inc., 1984), 31.

Job looked back on the effect of his losses and declared, "I do not have the strength to endure. I do not have a goal that encourages me to carry on" (Job 6:11 NLT). An affirmation helps us maintain focus in times of discouragement and setback. If God had a plan for the heroes of the Old and New Testaments, and even the pagan King Cyrus (Isaiah 45:1–5), formulated and recorded centuries before he was born, how much more does He have a plan for the life of every Christ-follower. I learned that a well written affirmation includes several ingredients: It is personal, looks to tomorrow and has the capacity to inspire me.

Mine includes favourite scripture verses as well as little slogans or insightful quotes. It speaks of a destiny for my life—not just filling in time till I die. It meets my need for meaning and purpose and helps me stay 'on course' when the 'winds of change' blow. It has been part of my devotional pattern over many years and is invaluable.[6]

Here are a couple of thoughts that make good sense:

- I would rather attempt to do something great and fail, than attempt to do nothing and succeed.[7]

- Again today, I exercise my great human freedom and choose my attitude regardless of the circumstances.[8]

- I have proven that any person "can fight the battle for just one day.

- It is only when I add the burdens of those two awful eternities, yesterday and tomorrow, that I tremble. It is not the experiences of today that drive me to distraction; it is the remorse or bitterness for something that happened yesterday or the dread of what tomorrow may bring."[9] I will therefore live one day at a time and take advantage of this precious moment of today.

---

[6] When you have finished this chapter take a moment to browse the sample in Appendix C.

[7] A calendar quote Robert Schuller read at a formative time in his life. *Move Ahead with Possibility Thinking* (New York: Doubleday Co.) 1967, 15.

[8] This is an adapted Viktor Frankl quote who is mentioned earlier in this chapter. Quote from Maxwell, *Your Attitude—Key to Success.* 31.

[9] Maxwell, *Your Attitude—Key to Success,* 117.

To begin thinking more positively and leading others to do the same, let me encourage you to follow the guidelines covered in the remainder of this chapter.

Imagination and radiance

In the Sermon on the Mount, Jesus helps us see the importance of guarding our minds. When He says that lusting and hating are the equivalent of breaking two of the Ten Commandments, He is speaking of the way that the imagination lies at the heart of living in true obedience to God. You will remember that I mentioned in Chapter 6 that sometimes the real difference between someone who has broken a rule, and one who has not, is whether or not they had an *opportunity* to do so without fear of being caught.

Dr Dobson commented in one of his writings that whenever a marriage breaks up because of unfaithfulness, the guilty party has imagined themselves doing the sin many times beforehand. Imagination is just as powerful as that. God's gift of a conscience informed by scripture greatly helps us resist these urges and imaginations. It is important to be sure the conscience is well trained and that we are listening to the voice of the Holy Spirit. Paul persecuted the church with a clear conscience at first, but gradually came to a point where God could confront him and he entered a whole new chapter of his life. (The words of Jesus: "It is hard for you to fight against my will" (Acts 26:14 NLT) are a clue that something had been happening in Paul's conscience, *before* the Damascus road appearance.)

Dr Glenn Clark developed a similar idea from Habakkuk 3:19, which is also found in Psalm 18:33. In his book *I will lift up Mine Eyes*, he describes an old gentleman who took an opportunity to share with one fellow passenger each train ride. He told his story about changing his way of thinking, to be like the hind. He writes,

> No animal has such perfect correlation of its front and rear feet as the deer. [They always track the back feet where the front feet were.] While the male deer, or the hart, is a wonder of sure-footedness, still more wonderful is the female, or the hind, which, while leading its young into hidden fastnesses, is the most perfect example of physical correlation that God has ever made.... *As the feet of the hind are to the mountains, so is the mind of man to the heights of life; and as the rear feet of the hind are to the front feet, so is the subconscious mind of man to*

the conscious mind." [He then quotes Proverbs 23:7]: 'As [a man] thinks in his heart so is he.'[10]

In my own life, one of the great discoveries in my search for holiness was that the key to the battle with temptation lies in the discipline of our imagination. It seems that many do not understand this. The advertising agencies know how to harness greed to the extent that a *Time* magazine article quoted Americans as "buying $1,300 worth of merchandise on credit for every $1,000 they earn".[11] We could write of 'obsessive compulsives', but the heart of the matter is greed. I have no doubt that greed is equally a problem in Australia?

> The key to the battle with temptation lies
> in the discipline of our imagination

Consider these scriptures which speak directly to this, and note the reference to the mind or imagination.

Daniel 1:8: "But Daniel purposed in his heart that he would not defile himself with the portion of the king's delicacies,[12] nor with the wine which he drank." It was a conscious choice, graciously communicated, but the starting place was his mind.

Romans 12:2: "Do not be conformed to this world, but be *transformed* by the renewing of your mind, that you may prove what is that good and acceptable and perfect will of God" (Italics added).

The Greek word translated 'transformed' is *metamorpho* from which we get our English word metamorphosis. It is used to describe the process as the chrysalis of the grub becomes a butterfly, or the transition from a tadpole to a frog. There is a complete change. That is the idea behind the verse. It is not like a change of mind at the shop, when after ordering fish and chips, you suddenly switch the order to a hamburger. Rather the mind is renewed with God's truth and we develop over time a different set of values and priorities.

---

[10] Clark, *I Will Lift Up Mine Eyes*, 21.
[11] William Backus and Marie Chapian, *Why Do I Do What I Don't Want to Do?* (Minneapolis, MN: Bethany House Publishers, 1984), 91.
[12] The Babylonians did not bleed the meat in accordance with scripture, so it was 'unclean' for Daniel.

The same word is used of Jesus when He was transfigured on the mountain (Matthew 17:2) and of believers in 2 Corinthians 3:18 where the change comes with time spent in the presence of God and letting His Holy Spirit work in us, "... bringing every thought into captivity to the obedience of Christ" (2 Corinthians 10:5). Paul informs the Corinthian readers that he guards his mind and he pictures the battle with which we are still familiar today. The reference to 'strongholds' applies to cleansing our mind with confession, guarding further input, and if necessary, directing evil to depart in the Name of Jesus.

Philippians 4:8-9: "Fix your thoughts on what is true and honourable and right. Think about things that are pure and lovely and admirable. Think about things that are excellent and worthy of praise. Keep putting into practice all you learned from me and heard from me and saw me doing, and the God of peace will be with you" (NLT). This verse comes in the 'I can' chapter of Paul's letter to the Philippian church where he speaks of ways the Christian life is an enabling experience. Take a moment to review the chapter and consider these 'I can' affirmations which I have adapted: I can

- Verse 1: love— "My beloved and longed-for brethren...."
- Verse 2: be a peacemaker— "I implore Euodia and ... Syntyche to be of the same mind...."
- Verse 3: be a helper— "I urge you also, true companion [unnamed] help...."
- Verse 4: be full of joy— "Rejoice...."
- Verse 5: be considerate— "Let your gentleness be known to all...."
- Verse 6: not worry— "Be anxious for nothing, but in everything by prayer...."
- Verse 6: pray transparently— "... let your requests be made known to God;"
- Verse 7: be at peace— "... the peace of God ... will guard your hearts...."
- Verse 8: think correctly—Let your mind dwell on things of God.
- Verse 9: be renewed in my mind—Meditate on a godly example.
- Verse 10: be grateful—He rejoiced in the Lord for their care.

- Verse 11: be content— "... I have learned in whatever state I am, to be content:"
- Verse 12: be flexible— "I know how to be abased, and I know how to abound..."
- Verse 13: do "all things through Christ who strengthens me."
- Verse 15: affirm others—He thanks them for their sharing.
- Verse 20: give glory to God.

Dr Maxwell Maltz[13] was a plastic surgeon who noticed that most people responded to his surgical skills with a fresh start and changed relationships. He comments that he also learned a lot from those who did not change. They seemed to have a mental picture of how they were, and, unless that was corrected, their behaviour remained the same. Maltz developed the term 'self-image', and this insight significantly changed modern psychology. His experience clearly shows that whenever there is a battle between the will and the imagination, the latter always wins.

I had an experience playing basketball with young adults on the Gold Coast some years back, when I foolishly agreed to participate in a game after not having played for many years. When the ball came my way, I headed for our goal but there was no-one from our team to whom I could pass it, and realised I would have to make the shot. Later, there was a penalty and again I had to shoot. I pictured myself sinking the ball in the hoop before making the attempt, and both times it was successful—much to my surprise, and the delight of friends who were watching.

This harnessing of the imagination must always be seen as a positive force. Reflect on the life of Joseph, especially the way he was cruelly mistreated by his brothers, Potiphar's wife, Potiphar himself, and later the butler. Surely, the dreams he had while still a youth of 17 were part of the explanation for his tenacity, his loyalty to God and his acting honourably. One sequence puts it this way:

Sow a thought, and you reap an act.
Sow an act, and you reap a habit.
Sow a habit and you reap a character.
Sow a character and you reap a destiny.[14]

[13] Maxwell Maltz, *Psycho-Cybernetics* (New York: Pocket Books, 1969).
[14] DeNeff, *Whatever Became of Holiness?* 112.

Do you have a picture in your mind of the calling of God upon your life? If so, keep it sharp and clear. If not, plan to take steps to discover your spiritual gifts, to develop the skills you will need and see yourself always as God's person serving Him effectively in the days to come. Keep the vision clear.

This principle has both negative and positive sides to it: negatively, if we focus on a sin this can actually make it harder to resist. On the other hand, a person preparing to preach or share a testimony, whether publicly or one-on-one, can use their imagination to picture themselves as God's representative, bringing His Word to people in an interesting and captivating way.

> Sow a character and you reap a destiny.

The freedom of forgiveness

One of the most special areas of ministry for me, both here in Australia and overseas, has been camps for teens and young adults, as well as for adults. I have learned that an area where we all struggle is in regard to forgiveness. Hence it would be rare for me not to address this issue at some point in each series of messages. Where possible, I have made a time (usually after a message on forgiveness) when participants can make a list of hurts they have received and forgive them, as well as a list of sins and hurts they have committed against God. When it is complete, they pray through the items extending and seeking forgiveness. Finally, they cancel as one would cancel an invoice and write diagonally Matthew 6:14 on hurts against themselves and 1 John 1:9 on hurts against God. The other significant part of the exercise is to burn the list (obviously in a place where there is no fire risk) after prayer. Before they do, I always tell them to '*watch it burn*' as it helps the subconscious get the message that the matter is dealt with and can be forgotten now that it is forgiven. When we speak of guarding our imagination, this helps us to leave the past in the past.

The result is that we can at last be freed from the destructive effects of past wounds. David Seamands is one of the most helpful writers in this regard, and he comments that we never forget anything that we experience.[15] It lives in our memory. He calls it the misery and grandeur of being human. He then goes on to write of the enormous effort involved in keeping painful memories which lie in the depth of our personalities below the surface. This is because they torment us and can result in our feeling constantly weary. The remedy is not just forgiveness but guarding the mind as we have outlined here. Beyond that, we want to ensure that the destructive pattern does not continue. Do not allow your mind to imagine yourself committing a sin. This self-discipline will begin to control your temptation and help you live a holy life. Remember Daniel's decision, making up his mind not to defile himself with the king's food (Daniel 1). We are to focus our minds on that which God wants for our life.

One day I discovered that my smartphone was not holding all the numbers of people I wanted to call, so I decided to erase some that I no longer required, leaving space on the phone's memory. It is the same idea. It also applies with life's disappointments and hurts. In Genesis, we read that Joseph found himself in a dark dungeon, and his emotions could easily have degenerated into depression, anger, bitterness and despair. A part of the secret of his life was that he did not allow the darkness that surrounded him in the cell to enter his heart. The light of the dream within him was kept burning bright and clear. There was no space for the darkness to enter and darken his spirit.

We live in a world desperate for genuinely changed people. Sadly, most people think only of changing others and very few think of changing themselves. The inner transformation of our lives is a goal worthy of our best effort.

> We live in a world desperate for genuinely changed people.

I have stressed the part God calls the Christian to play, because as we commit our lives to Him, He wants to help us. The issue is whether we are willing to be completely obedient, to set up a disciplined routine and live by it. Then we will please Him and He

---

[15] Seamands, *Putting Away Childish Things*, 17.

will be able to do exciting things through our lives in the days to come.

New research

Brad Huddleston[16] has done invaluable work on the impact of modern technology on the human brain. I cannot recommend his book too highly. He begins by quoting reliable authorities who indicate that we are facing a situation where people (especially children and teens) are becoming addicted to things like computer games and texts and it is actually *damaging* their brains.[17]

He notes that in the realm of education, children who are exposed to electronic data are likely to have shorter attention spans. By allowing every soft vibration of their phone to interrupt their study sessions, they are much slower and less efficient learners. He mentions that even the beep of the phone of the person near you can be a distraction which makes the study time less useful.

> There is a video titled 'I Forgot My Phone' that has been viewed almost 49 million times ... on YouTube.... In one scene, a group of eleven young adults are out together for a fun time of bowling. The scene opens with a female rolling the bowling ball down the alley and she then smiles excitedly when she knocks several pins down. When she turns around triumphantly with her arm in the air to get some high fives, no one is paying attention. All ten of her friends are staring into their smartphones. They are all together, but they are not 'together'. In other words, they are disconnected even though ten of them are physically sitting together.[18]

I have heard accounts of teens at school in a circle at lunch time but all are concentrating on their phone. Consider the peer pressure on Christian teens in that setting. Brad continues with stories of children asking for a parent to be relieved of their cell phone so that the parent will talk to *them*.[19]

---

[16] Brad Huddleston, *Digital Cocaine—A Journey Towards iBalance* (Vereeniging 1930 RSA: Christian Art Publishers. 2016). His website is www.bradhuddleston.com.
[17] Ibid., 29.
[18] Ibid., 31.
[19] Ibid., 34.

He addresses the issue of multitasking and demonstrates that the brain is less efficient when multitasking[20] because it does not settle to any task before jumping to the other. When there is incoming information, it provokes excitement which results in a squirt of a potentially addictive neurotransmitter called dopamine.[21] He continues with a similar picture on texting and Facebook. I was shocked to read that this addiction issue is so severe that South Korea considers it such a public health crisis that treatment is offered in approximately two hundred counselling centres and China has three hundred such centres. Sadly, there is also the heartbreaking addiction to self-harm.[22]

The data included in Chapter 5 of Huddleston's book shows that internet pornography has a detrimental effect on people's *brains* as well as their relationships. It includes the fact that 40 million Americans are regular users, and a shocking number of those are Christian men![23] There is little doubt that this lies behind the disastrous breakdown of marriages with broken lives. Sadly, women are now also being affected, with material which hooks them. Sexting and revenge pornography are also mentioned, with the sad results of their permissive presence in our society. The effect of this pornography addiction on the brain is described as comparable to cocaine and heroin addiction *combined*.[24] Huddleston reports that a huge number of Australians spend up to 35 hours a week watching on-line pornography and many men stay up late at night in the never-ending search for new pleasures, but *never being satisfied*.[25] They lose their love for their spouse, but the dream is empty.

We need to beware of the way the enemy starts small and lets evil gradually increase, rather like the person who thinks a little bit of pornography doesn't matter, when it does—the brain is actually damaged and the addictive process begun.[26] Huddleston quotes "an article from The Witherspoon Institute titled *The New Narcotic* [which] compared how Internet pornography addiction is similar to cocaine and heroin addiction combined":

---

[20] Ibid., 32–33.
[21] Ibid., 33.
[22] Ibid., 35–36. His data is well researched by qualified and reputable authorities.
[23] Ibid., 65–66.
[24] Ibid., 73.
[25] Ibid., 75.
[26] Ibid., 73.

Cocaine is considered a stimulant that increases dopamine levels in the brain. Dopamine is the primary neurotransmitter that most addictive substances release, as it causes a "high" and a subsequent craving for a repetition of the high, rather than a subsequent feeling of satisfaction by way of endorphins. Heroin, on the other hand, is an opiate, which has a relaxing effect. Both drugs trigger chemical tolerance, which requires higher quantities of the drug to be used each time to achieve the same intensity of effect.

Pornography, by both arousing (the "high" effect via dopamine) and causing an orgasm (the "release" effect via opiates), is a type of polydrug that triggers both types of addictive brain chemicals in one punch, enhancing its addictive propensity as well as its power to instigate a pattern of increasing tolerance. Tolerance in pornography's case requires not necessarily greater quantities of pornography but more novel pornographic content like more taboo sexual acts, child pornography, or sadomasochistic pornography.[27]

> The enemy starts small and lets evil gradually increase

A friend from Alabama told the following story. The policeman saw the African American boy coming home with some big fish.

"How'd you catch 'em Jimmy?" "I found some big worms under a rock." "Why are your hands bleeding?" "The worms were biting me as I put 'em on the hook." "Show me the worms that are left." One look and he raced the boy to the hospital—too late. The worms were baby rattle snakes.[28]

It may have been exciting in the short term, but it destroyed the boy, as is happening today with the misuse of the internet. Before leaving the issue of guarding our minds, the issue of computer games deserves mention.[29] Brad refers to Steve Jobs' family, noting that at meals no electronic devices were in evidence, nor permitted at

---

[27] http://www.thepublicdiscourse.com/2013/10/10846/ quoted by Huddleston, *Digital Cocaine*, 73–74.

[28] I am aware that some have questioned whether the account is accurate, or just a fable. Regardless, it illustrates a truth.

[29] Huddleston *Digital Cocaine*, 86.

homework time. He goes on to identify others in tech-Mecca Silicone Valley, who take a similar stand with their families. The gadgets were carefully monitored to prevent this addiction![30] Do they know something they are not telling us?

Paul speaks to this issue when he writes:

Remember that in a race everyone runs, but only one person gets the prize. You also must run in such a way that you will win. All athletes practise strict self-control. They do it to win a prize that will fade away, but we do it for an eternal prize. So I run straight to the goal with purpose in every step (1 Corinthians 9:24–26 NLT).

Summary of insights:

- Remember total consecration requires diligence in *all* areas.
- Never let an exception occur. No more "Just one more time...."
- Remember each decision to do what is right because it is right, especially when it is difficult, leads to growth and development of character and integrity.
- Guard your mind. The devil is a liar.
- Harness the imagination to overcome temptation, and be pure and true.

> As Christians we must face the issue of guarding our minds where evil and compromise are involved.

Our world will never be the same as it was in the past. The technological advances have made life more comfortable and provided ready access to information, including world missions, to previously closed countries, in amazing ways. However, as Christians we must face the issue of guarding our minds where evil and compromise are involved, whether in the areas of pornography or other addictions and vices. The first Baptist minister in Australia (John McKaeg) was destroyed by alcohol, and sadly, many ministries today are being wrecked by the violation of biblical principles. Psalm 124:7 describes the bird that escapes the hunter's trap. May we be wise enough to learn from the mistakes of others.

---

[30] Ibid., 102, 110.

A RADIANT CHARACTER

Chapter 11

Accountability—Supported by Friends

There are some things you cannot do alone, such as: water ski, wrestle, have a party, a sack race, play Marco polo, get married, or be a Christian. We must remember that a group of 'called out' ones (the church), is Jesus' idea. He initiated it to provide us with many benefits, one of which is accountability. The long history of civilizations has shown what governments become when there is no accountability; we call it a dictatorship. The use of the ballot box has come from the Reformation, and we have good reason to be grateful.

> Two people can accomplish more
> than twice as much as one....
> If one person falls, the other can
> reach out and help.

An anthropologist once asked a Hopi Indian who lived near the Grand Canyon why so many of their songs were about rain. The man explained that it is so scarce in his part of the world, and then added, "That's why so many of *your* songs are about love." In a world craving for intimacy and love, the experience of a small group is really important. The groups are like 'families within the local church family' to which, if possible, everyone should belong. It meets a need that we all have.[1] In our desire to be a more radiant character, the small group is extremely important. Consider the small group of young Jewish men in Babylon (Daniel 1:6, 2:17, 3:12) and the way they supported each other when the pressure came on to conform to the Babylonian lifestyle, food, etc and especially the worship of

---

[1] William Backus, *Finding the Freedom of Self-Control* (Minneapolis, MN: Bethany House Publishers, 1987), 156 mentions the value of sharing with another when trying to break a bad habit.

Nebuchadnezzar. It is echoed in the wisdom of Solomon: "Two people can accomplish more than twice as much as one…. If one person falls, the other can reach out and help. But people who are alone when they fall are in real trouble" (Ecclesiastes 4:9-10 NLT).

The example of Jesus

From the beginning of His ministry on earth, Jesus focussed on a small group of individuals. He used this most effective method to prepare and mould the future leaders of His church. He called the twelve to 'be with Him', eating, travelling, talking and praying with Him as He taught them. This small-group context in which the apostles were trained enabled them to be sent out to preach (Mark 3:14). They learned from Jesus' example, watching as He taught the crowds, healed the sick, answered opposition and dealt with genuine enquirers. They also received the benefit of His specific instructions and warnings as He taught them privately in the group.

Among the apostles there were three—Peter, James and John—who formed the inner core. They were present at significant points in Jesus' ministry—on the Mount of Transfiguration (Matthew 17:1–9); at the raising of Jairus' daughter (Mark 5:37); and in the Garden of Gethsemane (Matthew 26:37). In such a cell, learning and application of truth could be more intensive. These men were bound together by their shared experiences.

The small group around Jesus provided a perfect learning environment. It also provided a setting for mutual support for the apostles and for Jesus himself. The twelve were able to discuss among themselves the things they were learning from Jesus. Amidst the trauma and confusion of the first Easter, they met together for support. Jesus himself recognised the twelve as those who stood by Him in His trials (Luke 22:28). The promise that "where two or three are gathered together in My name, I am there in the midst of them" (Matthew 18:20) recognises this too.

The pattern of the early church

The record of the early church in Acts and in the Epistles follows the model of Jesus, and reflects a structure based on small groups of believers who met often in private houses. "They worshipped together at the Temple each day, met in homes for the Lord's Supper, and shared their meals with great joy and generosity" (Acts 2:46

NLT). They met to pray in their houses (Acts 1:12–13; 4:23–24; 12:12). Paul's greetings in his letters reveal this too. Households made up of new converts were the nucleus around which churches were established (Acts 16:14–15; 31–34; 18:7–8). Homes were also the setting for worship, preaching, teaching and fellowship (Acts 5:42; 20:7–8). Paul's comments in Romans 16:5 clearly reflect this pattern.

Accountability in a small group

Larry Crabb has said it so well: "The central task of community is to create a place that is safe enough for the walls to be torn down, safe enough for each of us to own and reveal our brokenness. Only then can the power of connecting do its job. Only then can the community be used of God to restore our souls."[2] Christianity is about relationship with God and with one another. Christ-followers have met in small groups for encouragement and support throughout church history. This aspect surfaced again in the Reformation and especially in the 18th century awakening. Michael Henderson quotes Whitefield who comments, "*My Brother Wesley acted wisely—the souls that were awakened under his ministry he joined in class, and thus preserved the fruit of his labour. This I neglected, and my people are a rope of sand.*" Henderson then adds this summary statement:

> The Wesleyan revolution [revival] is an illustration that long-lasting spiritual transformation is not the product of dynamic preaching or of correct doctrine. It comes only through serious disciple-building, in keeping with Christ's Great Commission to 'go into all the world and make disciples.' The class meeting which Wesley developed was the instrument by which preaching and doctrine were harnessed into spiritual renewal. It carried the revolution.[3]

In many ways, when Wesley's converts met with other Christians and confessed their sins, they were obeying a scripture which many Bible-believing Christians ignore— "Confess your sins to each other and pray for each other so that you may be healed" (James 5:16

---

[2] Larry Crabb, *The Safest Place on Earth—Where People Connect and Are Forever Changed* (Nashville, TN: W Publishing Group a division of Thomas Nelson, 1999), 11.
[3] D. Michael Henderson, *John Wesley's Class Meeting—A Model for Making Disciples* (Nappanee IN: Francis Asbury Press of Evangel Publishing House, 1997), 31.

NLT).[4] For some this mutual ministry no doubt took place one-on-one, but as the revival spread, and numbers increased, small groups became the only way to provide both support and accountability.

As they did this, faithfully and regularly, they were helped to overcome sin in their lives, but, if this mutual ministry was to achieve its purpose, the sharing had to be safeguarded to ensure confidentially and the context kept small. Wesley's groups were also a forerunner of the Alcoholics Anonymous (AA) movement which was founded when Bill Wilson, who had been sober for six months, went on a business trip and a significant deal fell over. Feeling discouraged, he heard the noise from a nearby bar and headed in that direction, only to realise that, rather than a drink, what he needed was another alcoholic—someone who would understand the pressure he was facing, and encourage him to 'hold on'. Dr Smith became that friend—able to hold him accountable, and the ministry of AA was 'on its way'.

> You are as sick as your sickest
> secret, and you will remain
> sick as long as it stays a secret.

Their pamphlet comments: "Becoming sober is 90% about honesty and 10% about alcohol.... You are as sick as your sickest secret, and you will remain sick as long as it stays a secret." While on that topic I believe I would be negligent if I failed to mention that alcohol remains the cause of enormous heartache in our society, and as Christians we do have a responsibility for our weaker brothers.[5] This is a book about a godly lifestyle, and today's church needs to face this issue squarely. Sadly today's Western church has forgotten this and moved to affirm moderate drinking. In discussing this, people have quoted to me Paul's advice to young Timothy to "use a little wine for your stomach's sake and your frequent infirmities."[6] They seem to have missed the point that he is simply saying that it is OK for *medicinal* purposes. The comment would have been unnecessary had Timothy not been a total abstainer. I well

---

[4] Note the dimension of healing associated with the group.
[5] Romans 14: 7–14, 1 Corinthians. 8: 9–13.
[6] 1 Timothy 5:23.

remember a man sadly telling me he had his first 'drink' with a minister, and now wished he had never started.[7] Henry Lawson, one of our most famous poets, laughed at the 'Wowsers', but later was tragically destroyed by his addiction to alcohol. It is an area where we need to have convictions, even if they are unpopular.

Permit me to add a word to pastors and leaders: Your personal stance on this issue will have an impact on your hearers. Paul's word is timely "Don't tear apart the work of God over what you eat. Remember, there is nothing wrong with these things in themselves. But it is wrong to eat anything if it makes another person stumble. Don't eat meat or drink wine or do anything else if it might cause another Christian to stumble" (Romans 14:20–21 NLT).

Speaking of the importance of accountability and the tragedy of unconfessed sin, Gordon MacDonald quotes *The Boston Globe* in 1984, which told the tragic story of the drowning of an 8-year-old boy while hunting for golf balls. The three older ones said he had slipped into the pool. It was two years before the secret was uncovered that one of the others had pushed him in. During this time, all three had "suffered emotional instability, according to their parents, police, and their own stories. Their distraught parents say the boys are withdrawn and have nightmares. They are no longer friends."[8]

Bill Hull has made an outstanding contribution to the church in our day and he speaks of pseudo-transformation, which basically is just good habits without the deep inner conviction of God. He adds:

The church's default settings must be changed. How much longer can we stomach the reality that our work is fraudulent? How much longer will we allow people to think that sin management is acceptable? I raise the white flag of surrender to my sin; I just sin and confess, sin and confess, sin and confess, without expecting victory."[9]

He goes on to quote George Barna's study of the general Christian populace, with these conclusions:

---

[7] A police officer friend who deals with drug related issues, commented to me that alcohol is still the most abused drug in Australia. He affirmed that this can be backed up from the Australian Drug Foundation.
[8] MacDonald, *Rebuilding Your Broken World*, 82. He heads the chapter "The Pain of Secret Carrying".
[9] Hull, *Choose the Life*, 26.

... about 52 percent of Christians are making some effort to grow spiritually, but they are inconsistent and get limited results for their efforts. They are more inclined to read a devotional book, participate in a prayer group, or study an outline of their pastor's sermon, with only 17 percent willing to meet weekly with two or three others for accountability.[10]

This small-group mentoring context is the missing part. He affirms that we only allow into our lives the activities that fit our schedule, with the result that we are still our own master. He goes on to say: "To be a disciple as described by Jesus requires a person to submit himself or herself to a more mature follower of Jesus. Unless you have done so, you are not following Jesus in the way He desired."[11]

A little-known facet of Wesley's small groups is the way his *select societies* and *band* groups both went beyond the 'class meeting' basic model and included this deeper level of both mentoring and being mentored.[12] A mentor is like a personal spiritual coach who is always encouraging us to "do what [we] don't want, so [we] can become what [we] want to be."[13]

In nations where Christians are persecuted, house churches are again one of the few relatively safe places for believers to meet. The church in China and the Middle East has grown amazingly under such difficult conditions. Where resources and training are limited, small groups led by lay people are able to multiply the work of a trained pastor so that more lives can be changed. In South Korea, some of the world's largest churches are built on a structure of cell groups which meet in different parts of the city. In Australia's past, the Methodist laymen on the goldfields in Victoria used circuits and small groups so effectively that, even though Methodism was not begun in this country until almost twenty-five years after the First Fleet arrived and had none of the homeland advantages afforded the

---

[10] Ibid., 27.

[11] Ibid., 36.

[12] The sharing and mentoring was always same-sex for obvious reasons.

[13] Bill Hull, *The Disciple Making Pastor—The Key to Building Healthy Christians in Today's Church* (Grand Rapids, MI: Fleming H. Revell, 1997) quotes the coach of the Dallas Cowboys, Tom Landry's definition, 91.

other bigger denominations,[14] they were larger in the mining towns than all the others *combined*.[15]

Here is a touching account from our Australian past of the prayers and passion of the early Wesleyans, as well as the place of the small group supporting their witness. John Coles preached at the Melbourne jail and wanted to meet Ned Kelly, the notorious outlaw. The governor said, "No, he's Catholic." Coles' small group prayed. The next time Coles preached, Kelly heard the message from his cell and wanted to meet him. Several meetings took place during Sept.–Oct. 1880. Here are extracts from Coles' journal entries:

.... I refused to hear anything from him about his bushranging exploits, but I kept him to this—that we might die any moment. "Do not think, Kelly, for one moment that it is out of any foolish curiosity to see you that I have sought these interviews; nothing of the sort. Indeed, I wish I could be spared the pain of seeing an intelligent young man like you in such an awful position. My sole object in speaking to you is to impress on you the fact that you have a soul to be saved, or for ever lost; that Christ died for the chief of sinners. If you will but be sorry for your sin and confess it to God and ask for mercy for Christ's sake, He will have mercy on you."

Coles and Kelly then knelt side by side and prayed together. Upon standing Kelly crossed himself and thanked the preacher for his ministry.[16]

Vital small groups are also an important facet of growing churches today. In America, surveys have consistently shown that the churches that are growing are those where members belong to small groups providing nurture, acceptance and meaning. Just as the body needs bones, and a building needs a framework, our faith needs a stable context. Hull's book *Building High Commitment in a Low Commitment World* is profound. He correctly affirms that "You can't make disciples without accountability, and you cannot have accountability without structure. If a church is going to develop

---

[14] The Catholics in Ireland, Anglicans in England, and Presbyterians in Scotland, all had the smile of their respective governments—not so the Methodists.
[15] Geoffrey Searle, *The Golden Age—A History of the Colony of Victoria 1851–1861* (Parkville, Victoria: Melbourne University Press, 1963), 342–343 quoted by Lindsay Cameron, *Methodism Reborn—The Wesleyan Methodist Church in the South Pacific* (Perth, Australia: Cypress Project, 2017), 72.
[16] Extracted from www.sonlife.com.au/index.php?option=com...view.../Ned+Kelly...

people, then the question the leaders must consider is 'what kind of structure?'"[17] But not every kind of small group provides it.

We do well to remember how the geese were designed to fly in a 'V formation', adding a greater flying range for the flock than when each bird flies alone. The single goose quickly returns to the formation within the flock when it recognises the additional thrust that comes from alignment with others. We can go further, faster, and easier, going together. The truth is that loneliness is epidemic in our society and social media has in some instances made it worse, as the person who writes to them does not always match the image conveyed. The face-to-face part is missing. John Stott refers to the "phenomenal growth of the church in many parts of the world" in the last century, but sums it up in three words, "growth without depth". He quotes a leader from South Asia who identified the numerical growth and added "there is a huge problem with lack of godliness and integrity."[18]

> Loneliness is epidemic in our society and social media has in some instances made it worse.

Martin Robinson has analysed our society's crisis well when he says:

> The radical individualism of the secular West causes those who imbibe such a culture to have enormous problems with such matters as commitment and the building of long-term relationships. It doesn't take much imagination to consider what takes place in a local church when strong commitment in relationships is absent. Division, upset, unhappiness, rumour, refusal to work with others followed by an all-too-easy departure for another church. That familiar process has produced many spiritual wanderers who have a tendency to move from church to church, never really becoming committed in any situation before finally dropping out of church completely.... The small-group context is almost

---

[17] Bill Hull, *Building High Commitment in a Low Commitment World* (Grand Rapids, MI: Fleming H. Revell, 1995), 171.
[18] Stott, *The Radical Disciple—Wholehearted Christian Living*, 43–44.

certainly the most helpful means of exploring what it means to be committed to one another in relationships. [This will also greatly enrich our personal devotional life.][19]

Appendix B[20] outlines a model which came from my research into the 18th century small groups in England, which so greatly contributed to the spiritual awakening of that time. Wesley's model continued to greatly impact the UK for more than 100 years and here in Australia, especially during the 19th century. Many dear friends have helped me identify the principles and adapt the model for today, and I am convinced it was the key to the remarkable health and warmth of the churches I served, especially the one where I was pastor for 10 years in Brisbane. It has also been a vital part of the 'restoring'[21] of churches I have served since. Obviously, it is not the *only* way to enjoy accountability but, whatever way we do it, the need must be met for a life to be changed.

> The small-group context is almost certainly the most helpful means of exploring what it means to be committed to one another in relationships.

Part of the rebuilding of people in a small group includes the need to give assurance that the sharing will be safe, because meaningful relationships require mutual respect with regard to confidences. We used a written covenant to allow participants to understand the expectations. When I am sometimes asked if such a document is necessary, the answer really depends on the *purpose* of the group. If it is just a religious club of friends occasionally encouraging each other, it is less crucial. But once we find ourselves facing life's struggles, we like to share with friends, whether to seek advice, prayer, or just have a shoulder to cry on. It is when this sharing happens on any regular basis that the idea of a covenant becomes important if we want to minimize hurts and enhance our growth.

---

[19] Martin Robinson, *To Win the West* (Crowborough, East Sussex: Monarch Publications, 1996), 212–213.
[20] It's well worth reading if you are serious about this.
[21] This meant helping a struggling church identify what was stifling its growth and correct it, enabling progress to resume.

A covenant (whether written, or simply an understanding stated corporately at the beginning of the year), makes the group a safer place. It defines expectations and provides security based on trust. Members can know what to expect. The group may be under a local church or an interdenominational gathering. Either way, adopting a covenant helps us make progress. One study has concluded that "In order for anyone to grow, there must be a safe, risk-free environment."[22] Bill Hull expands upon this conclusion, commenting:

> Repentance and confession are linked to trust in others. Can I be real? Can I be vulnerable? Can I submit myself to these people? Unless the community provides a safe environment that promotes trust, people will not open up. Unless people open up, transformation will be largely absent, which explains a lot of the problems the church is facing.[23]

Hull is writing about a structure for Church life to develop a 'radiant character'. It will not always be easy but it is worth pursuing, especially if we long for personal and national spiritual awakening.

One final comment—please remember small groups are about relationships and thus the social structure of the church will be affected. Please do not try to just impose this idea on your church. Such initiatives need to be carefully implemented under the guidance of leadership. An 'ad hoc' start may be enjoyable at first, but it will bring problems down the track without diligent preparation at the start.

---

[22] Thrall, McNicol, and McElrath, *The Ascent of a Leader* (San Francisco: Jossey-Bass, 1999), Chapter 11, quoted by Hull, *Choose the Life*, 133.
[23] Hull, Choose the Life, 133.

Chapter 12

Investing in Others

It has been well said that "when the chess game is over, the pawns, rooks, kings and queens all go back into the same box." Perhaps it reflects my stage in the journey of life, but I sometimes reflect on the big picture of life on our planet. The media have pictures of famous people; but then I think of other people, whose names are known only to God and a few friends. They are doing a marvellous job in some remote location sharing hope and meaning with a 'people' group.[1] So what does it mean to discover a destiny? How important is the message of holiness outlined in this book, and where does it fit? Is it simply so we will have a happier ride? Surely not! The Lord desires to anoint each of our lives to make a difference for good in our world, and the key is making this message and experience our own, in relationship with Him.

> The Lord desires to anoint each of our lives
> to make a difference for good in our world.

I have always been impressed by this quote from Wesley's *Journal*:

> From long experience and observation, I am inclined to think that whoever finds redemption in the blood of Jesus—whoever is justified—has the choice of walking in the higher or the lower path. I believe the Holy Spirit at that time sets before him the "more excellent way", and incites him to walk therein—to choose the narrowest path in the narrow way—to aspire after the heights and depths of holiness—after the entire image of God. But if he does not accept this offer, he insensibly declines into the lower order of Christians; he still goes on in what may be called a good way, serving God in his

---

[1] We usually call them 'missionaries' but in fact we are all missionaries to our culture.

degree, and finds mercy in the close of life through the blood of the covenant.[2]

My prayer for you is that you will choose the higher, more excellent way, letting nothing hinder you from being filled and controlled by the Holy Spirit, and discover His plan and destiny for your life.

Thus, the decisions before you as the reader at this point are:

- Have I taken the step of making a total commitment to the Lord, realising it will cost me, but be well worth it?
- Am I prepared to establish a routine characterised by a guarded mind and a small group or close friend for accountability?
- What will I do with the insights I have gleaned to influence positively the lives of others?

The story is told of a Jewish rabbi in Russia who was so discouraged that he went out into the streets one night, and without realising it, stumbled into an army base. He was snapped out of his melancholy mental ramblings by the harsh voice of a guard who asked, "Who are you and what are you doing here?" His brain responded very quickly with a question. "What do they pay you each day?" When the surprised official replied, the rabbi said, "I'll double it if you'll ask me that question every day. I need to remember my answer." We all need to know *our* answer to the guard's questions.

In Chapter 10, we briefly touched on the value of a personal affirmation. I would urge you to develop your own. You may like to include some of the ideas in that chapter. Remember there is a sample in Appendix C to get you started.

Josh McDowell[3] tells of a man whose job is 'head-hunting', which is shorthand for recruiting executive staff from other companies. He says that at the interview, they take off their coats, loosen their ties, and have a friendly chat including hobbies, footy, family; then when the guy is relaxed, suddenly he leans over, looks him square in the eye, and asks him, "So what's your purpose in life?" McDowell comments that while sadly many are speechless at the question, he

[2] Cook, *New Testament Holiness*, 6.
[3] McDowell, *His Image, My Image*, 153.

was impressed when one man without blinking an eye said: "To go to heaven and take as many people with me as I can." That's grand!

Part of my purpose in writing this book is to offer readers the opportunity to become more like Jesus now, enjoying the challenging, abundant life He promised here, and by the impact of a godly life to encourage as many people as possible to join the adventure, both here on earth and beyond. I believe that too many people have made the commitment, but did not know the skills or importance of following through with a godly lifestyle.

I remember a Sunday night, 8th April 1956, when I made a choice to follow the Lord. I deepened that in August 1962 at a high school camp. On both occasions, I was counselled to read the Bible every day. While the earlier reading resolution lasted only a couple of weeks, the latter decision continues to this present day.

While doing ministry tours away from home, I call my wife several times a day. Those calls are not unlike my prayers each day. In addition to a time of devotions at the start, there are many conversations with the Lord. They include admiration: "What an awesome God You are, designing my hand to be able to do that manoeuvre." Or, "What a stunning panorama. I praise You Lord!" They also include cries for help when things are not going well; and when I can't find something, I find myself turning to the Lord—that happens often. Other prayers include requests to bless and help people who come to my mind. They may be friends, or public figures or an international situation where I pray wisdom for the decision-makers and protection and strength for Christians in the world's trouble spots.

Recently, I attended the movie *The Case for Christ,* on the adult life of Lee Strobel, which I very much enjoyed. There were many scenes where, as I watched, I was praying for audiences around the world who would see the film, that the Lord would take that scene and speak to those He wanted to reach through the movie. As I read an internet news report of a professor claiming that the Bible was just a 'collection of legends', I prayed God would help the people reading the drivel in that report to 'see through it' and for the author to 'see the light'.

All these 'calls on the Royal telephone' are part of my relationship with the Lord. They remind me indirectly that I live in *His* world and that He is at work behind the scenes. It adds zest to my life to remember that for the Christian nothing happens that God has not both anticipated and already planned to use for good.

Chapters 2 and 3 described some who had such a change that others noticed and many 'joined in the challenge'. Dr John Brasher of the National Holiness Association in the USA spoke of how he, as a young theological student, attended one of Brengle's meetings. He said:

> [I was] armed with all the arguments against the doctrine I knew he would preach.... But even as I listened, ... I became captivated by his face, his voice, his mannerisms. I had found the answer to my arguments, not in his logic, which probably was entirely sound, but in his very attitude, in his projection of God's glory. That night I found the blessing. That night I commenced a life of holiness that has been sufficient for more than half a century.[4]

If you follow through with the ideas and biblical principles we have considered in this book, life will be an adventure for you, and you will have the thrill of helping others too.

A friend reminded me that on judgement day, we will be questioned in three areas:

1) What have you done about the wrong things of which you are guilty? That is about salvation.
2) What have you done with the gifts and opportunities you were given? That is about stewardship.
3) Whom have you brought with you? That is about witness.

> God didn't just change what I *do*,
> He changed what I *want* to do.

I always enjoy watching Ravi Zacharias presenting or when in debate. My favourite occasion was when he was asked by an atheist, "Suppose I were to convince you that God is not there, I'm interested in what sin you're really wishing you could commit, but you're afraid that the Almighty would know about it?" Ravi's reply was brilliant.

---

[4] Agnew, *Transformed Christians*, 67–68.

He said, "You don't understand. When I became a Christian, God didn't just change what I *do,* He changed what I *want* to do."[5]

That is the wonderful reality of the holy life. There is a freedom to which Jesus referred when He said, "Therefore if the Son makes you free, you shall be free indeed" (John 8:36).

Another story I heard quite some years ago comes from Russia about the terrible days when people were interrogated and mistreated: An engineer whose careless comment had landed him in jail, was being interrogated. He entered the room, sat down and blew his nose loudly. The officer demanded, "Why did you sit without my permission?" He replied, "It is better to walk than to run, and better to sit than to stand!" The officer replied, "Don't you realise that I have power over you?" Still seated, the prisoner added, "You have no power over me at all. You can't touch my wife and child. They're already dead. You can't take my property from me as I have already lost it all. I suggest that when you want to control someone, don't take everything from him, because when a man loses everything, he becomes free in a new way."

Thankfully, we probably will not find ourselves in that kind of situation, but the good news of the gospel is that when we see everything we have as *His*, there is a new level of freedom which is liberating. We are simply stewards caring for the property of Another Whom we love and serve.

The truth is that when God gives you a vision of His calling on your life, it is so you can persevere when the times of suffering and loneliness come. Consider Joseph's life as we read it in Genesis 37–50. He was repeatedly mistreated, lied about and no doubt felt desperately alone and forsaken, yet all these experiences were preparing him for a destiny that would take God's purpose for His chosen people further forward, save many lives, and be an inspiration to millions in the future.

Part of our calling will be encouraging others, and I do not mean flattery because it is insincere and damages all concerned. Rather, honest appreciation, noting and affirming people's qualities along the way, is a skill to be learned. As I look back on my years of ministry, I believe it has blessed others as I have sought to express

---

[5] Ravi Zacharias, DVD: *Is There Meaning in Evil and Suffering?* (Presented by the Faith and Science Lecture Forum in Atlanta GA).

genuine encouragement and friendship. When I was in upper high school, a very kind subject master took me aside one afternoon and asked me very directly, "Has it dawned on you that you are the most unpopular kid in the school?" She required me to read *How to Win Friends and Influence People* by Dale Carnegie. It really helped me, as I learned how to live by the Golden Rule in today's world.[6] I mention it here because no amount of spirituality will compensate for poor people-skills. Sadly, there have been times when I have seen unnecessary damage done to others by failure of leaders at this level. If you are called to make a difference in our world, that book is worth reading because his insights will help you avoid unnecessary pain and frustration.

I was counselling a young high schooler who was being given a hard time by one of his teachers—an atheist. When he casually mentioned the man's name (an unusual one), I was stunned. That man had been my Sunday school teacher many years before! Part of our mission is to be able to share answers to life's questions on the reliability of the Bible, the origin and meaning of life, and especially the 'why' of suffering and how to cope, with a certainty of faith. We need to be able to pass them on to others.[7] The church today needs not only to reach new people but also to hold the ones we already have.

> The church today needs
> not only to reach new people
> but also to hold the ones we already have.

While it is God's will for all to be filled with the Holy Spirit, it does not mean we all have the same gifts or calling. The whole thrust of 1 Corinthians 12–14 is that the Lord distributes different abilities to different members of His body, the church, (though we *all* need the most excellent thing—love). Not everyone is called to be an overseas missionary, and not every pastor is gifted to be a senior pastor. We need to discover and faithfully use our unique mix of gifts. Luther is

---

[6] "Do for others what you would like them to do for you" (Matthew 7:12 NLT).
[7] www.creation.com is invaluable in this regard since well researched answers, by godly and qualified people, to so many of these questions are available.

the one who introduced the idea of our employment as a *vocation* or calling, whether in a trade, agriculture, or a people profession.

I am convinced that the dream in the heart of God for our world in our lifetime, is a mighty spiritual awakening. He is so sovereign and so powerful that He can make even the plans and actions of evil people contribute in more ways than one. The first way is that they modify circumstances which God can use to extend His kingdom. A good biblical example is the way the division of the kingdom after Solomon meant that many godly Jews migrated south from the northern tribes and Judah's life as an independent nation continued for more than a century after the fall of Samaria. A relatively recent saga was the expulsion of missionaries from China, after the Communist takeover in 1949. It resulted in church planting across South East Asia by a wonderful team of dedicated workers who were already expert in Chinese culture, and God was well able to grow a healthy church in China. As I have commented earlier, we need to see God at work at such times. He really is sovereign. Above all, we see the wonderful way God used the awful tragedy of the cross, arranged by evil individuals to bless His people and through them, the whole world.

The second way our Lord harnesses the actions of His opponents is that He uses the sufferings they cause us, to refine our character (Daniel 12:10).[8] As we forgive those who have wronged us, persist in the face of trials, and look for ways to pass on the message of meaning, purpose and hope which has been entrusted to us, the kingdom of God moves forward.

> He uses the sufferings
> to refine our character

As a fielder in cricket, when you move to catch the ball, there is a dimension of anticipation. You watch the angle, subconsciously figure where it is likely to land, and start moving to the spot. Similarly, playing chess, you anticipate your opponent's likely next moves and shift your pieces accordingly. I learned it in the Scouts with the motto 'Be prepared'. It has been a very useful habit whether in parenting, driving a car, or leading a ministry. So, what does it

---

[8] I have given this more detail in Chapter 8.

mean as we come to the last pages of this book? Can you share a dream of a changed world in our lifetime—of a changed *you* as you put these biblical principles into action? I can truly say I have sought to trust God's leading in my life and, apart from some of my foolish blunders in the past, I have no regrets.

Although I have not emphasised the place of prayer in this book, it is *very* important. I don't understand why the Lord made this communication avenue open to us, but I am sure it is related to the spiritual battle in which we are engaged. It means we may at times feel hopeless, but we are never helpless. When we see an opportunity or a need, we can participate in the process by upholding the people involved before God. Just *how* He answers will sometimes be a surprise, but always a step forward for His plans. I remind myself that Jesus is alive making intercession, as He is praying for us (Hebrews 7:25) and "the Spirit Himself makes intercession for us with groanings which cannot be uttered" (Romans 8:26). In your praying, please do not miss the call to repentance, at the end of Chapter 5.

John Wesley said, "Give me one hundred preachers who fear nothing but sin and desire nothing but God, and I care not a straw whether they be clergymen or laymen. Such alone will shake the gates of hell and set up the kingdom of heaven upon earth."[9] Surely, that is what happened at Pentecost. I believe it can happen again, in our day. May the Lord revive us again, and may He bless you, as you find His fullness and discover the part He has for you to play. It is all about discovering our destiny—a spiritual awakening and moving forward for God.

Paul's letter to the Ephesian church has a cluster of instructions, one of which is "walk as children of the light" (Ephesians 5:8). I wrote in the margin of my Bible decades ago, 'walk radiantly'. May the insights of this book be an encouragement to you to strive for a radiant character as your response to God's love and plan for your life. Edwin Markham is known for his quote: "Great it is to believe the dream, as we stand in youth by the starry stream; but a greater thing is to [press on] through, and say at the end, the dream is true!"

---

[9] www.wesley.nnu.edu/john-wesley/the-letters-of-john-wesley/wesleys-letters-1777/" \l "Fifteen".

Appendix A

Definitions

The English language, like any other, is subject to variation as the years pass and words change their meaning; For example, 'let' meant 'prevented' four hundred years ago. Today, it means 'to permit'. The word 'discriminating' was a compliment fifty years ago, but today is a criticism. 'Prevent' meant to 'go ahead', now it means to restrain. 'Wicked' has also changed its meaning completely.

It will be worth taking time to look at definitions, and at misconceptions that have made our task of communicating the message more challenging. The list will not try to cover every term, but only those where confusion may exist and which are important parts of the teaching.

Conversion	Confessing our sin and self-centredness, accepting God's grace and becoming fully committed to Jesus as Lord and Master of our lives. Sin includes rebellious attitudes as well as actions.
Preparing Grace	Since we humans are unable to save ourselves or even think of repenting, God's preparing grace enables us to do so. T. C. Hammond declares that, "The Reformation Divines were almost unanimous in support of this doctrine".[1]
Sanctify	The word means 'set apart for a special purpose'. It is frequently used in the Old Testament, in association with the sacrificial system and God's desire for His people. The New Testament continues this usage. There are two aspects—set apart *from* sin, and set apart *for* God's service. It could be replaced with 'make holy'. The word is often used in older writings on holiness but is not in common usage today.

---

[1] T. C. Hammond, *In Understanding Be Men* (London: IVF Publishing, fifth edition, 1954), 143.

Entire sanctification Sometimes called 'full salvation'	This is the position of *complete* devotion to God (1 Thessalonians 5:23). The whole personality is integrated and preserved blameless. It was a prayer Paul expected to be answered for his friends. While it *is* a scriptural term, it has been misunderstood, and may more helpfully be replaced with 'filled with the Holy Spirit'.
	Full salvation has been used by some 19th century writers, but clearly it implies more than conversion.
Remorse	Feelings of serious regret for an attitude or action without an intent to change. (Judas felt 'remorse' and hanged himself.)
Repentance	Feelings of regret and penitence about an attitude or action, *accompanied by a desire and willingness to change.* (Peter felt 'repentance' and made a fresh start, becoming a great apostle of Christ.) This was treated in depth in Chapter 5.
Sin	At its core, sin is rebellion against God's right as our Creator to tell us how to live. The central issue touches on the will, set in rebellion against Him—*I want my way*. It can be either an act, or an attitude,[2] taking the form of active disobedience or simply ignoring God. Some Christians think of sin as *any falling short of the divine standard of perfection.* While this is quite compatible with our definition of God as perfect, holy, and separate from sin, it does not fit the Bible. More than once, Jesus told people to 'go and sin no more'; for example, the woman taken in adultery (John 8:11). Obviously, He was not saying that she should henceforth be perfect in every way, but rather start living in obedience to God from here on. Wesley defined sin as a *wilful transgression of a known law of God.* Such a definition excludes human failings, and allows the command of Jesus to be obeyed. The whole purpose of this book has been to enable you to come to a point where you are living a life that is fully pleasing to God, and a blessing to your neighbour—a radiant character.

---

[2] Wesley saw the above as the primary sense but he did recognise the Reformed definition of sin as applying in a secondary sense. There is a further comment in Chapter 6.

Infirmity	An illness, or state of being infirm, feeble, frail, a personal failing or defect. It has its foundation in an *involuntary lack* of power, whereas a sin is *a wilful misuse* of the present light and power we have. This means there is no guilt where there is neither choice nor any decision of the will. It is not a sin to be sick, make a mistake when adding figures, or genuinely forget to keep an appointment.
Temperament	A basic trait which blends with experience to form personality. Temperament includes the aspects of personality pertaining to *moods* and ways of doing things, for example, introverted or extroverted, time or event-oriented. Being filled with the Holy Spirit does not mean we will all have the same personality.
Holiness	This can, and does refer to the very heart of God's character.[3] Also, when believers are filled with the Holy Spirit, it begins a whole new chapter in their Christian lives. That is the focus of this book. I tend to use the word *holiness* as shorthand for that experience and the life lived from then on.
Sanctification	Biblical term meaning the same as 'holiness', but rarely used today. Other terms that have been used over the years include: 'Sealing with the Holy Spirit', 'Second blessing', 'Deeper life', 'Modern Pentecost' and a more recent one is, 'Undivided Heart'. Wesley's term 'Christian perfection' or 'perfect love' are sometimes more helpful.

An important clarification on what it means to be filled with the Holy Spirit

The 20th century saw another stream of Christianity emerge with roots in the holiness movement of the 19th century, and that concerns the practice of speaking in tongues. For our study, the important thing to note is that many see the use of this gift as the sign that a person has been 'filled with the Holy Spirit'.[4]

---

[3] All the others depend on that. Without His holiness, His love becomes mere sentiment, His justice is meaningless, His mercy isn't needed, His goodness lacks purpose and direction, and becomes mere benevolence, and as for His power without holiness, it is terrifying. This summarises material from DeNeff, *Whatever Became of Holiness?* 21–23. His insights are well worth reading in more detail.

[4] I do not find this a helpful approach, since 1 Corinthians 12:30 clearly rules out the idea that every believer has *every* gift. The Greek has a very precise word which

The practice has been linked with the rapid expansion of the church in the last century or so, and all believers celebrate that good news. This book has attempted to explain and encourage every reader to be filled with the Holy Spirit, so I have used that phrase often. I am not here debating the 'pro's and cons' of the gift of speaking in tongues, or wanting to belittle anyone's experience, but clarifying that biblically, it is not the *sign* of that filling.

The day of Pentecost included the speaking in other languages (*dialektos* in Greek from which we get our modern word 'dialect'). These were known languages and the text identifies sixteen national groups from which listeners heard them speak the "wonderful works of God" in their own tongue (Acts 2:9–11). God also used this sign to confirm the opening of the door of faith to the Gentiles, when Peter preached at the home of Cornelius (Acts 10:44–46). The only other mention in the book of Acts is in Ephesus with a group of the disciples of John the Baptist (Acts 19:5–7). In the case of these two references, the sign served as a seal or confirmation to Jewish Christians that this group was accepted by God and may be included in the church. Unhappily, some confuse the utterances of the modern movement (sometimes called a 'prayer language') with the above-mentioned signs to the Jewish Christians.

The only other New Testament mention of tongues concerns the multi-lingual city of Corinth, where Paul had to correct a number of abuses (1 Corinthians 12–14). It is helpful to contrast the Acts experience with the Corinthian one, as there are some very significant differences. The following table is adapted from data by Michael Griffiths, former Director of the Overseas Missionary Fellowship, in his book *Three Men Filled with the Spirit*.[5]

---

indicates when a "No" answer is expected and Paul used that form six times in verses 29–30.
[5] Michael C. Griffiths, *Three Men Filled with the Spirit—The Gift of Tongues; Must It Divide Us?* (London: Overseas Missionary Fellowship, 1969), 13.

Pentecost	Corinth
In Jerusalem, *all* 120 spoke in tongues [Acts 2:1–4].	At Corinth 'not all' spoke in tongues [1 Cor. 12:30].
'Tongues' were understood by many, or most (Acts 2:7–11).	'Tongues' were understood by none, except the interpreter [1 Cor. 14:2,3].
They were spoken to people (Acts 2:6).	They were spoken to God (1 Cor. 14:2).
No interpreter needed (Acts 2:8).	Forbidden unless interpreted (1 Cor. 14:28).
[There was perfect harmony (Acts 2:1)].	[There was confusion and disorder (1 Cor. 14:33,40)].
[Preaching was central (Acts 2:14–40)].	[Preaching (prophecy) was coming a poor second to 'tongues' (1 Cor. 14:27; cf. 14:19)].
[The unsaved were challenged and converted (Acts 2:37–41)].	[Likelihood that the unsaved would think 'tongues-speakers' were mad (1 Cor. 14:23)].
Brought salvation to others.	Edified only the speakers (1 Cor. 14:4).

Griffiths' conclusion seems amply justified: "There is therefore a very strong case for the view that the Pentecost event was *different* from the normal occurrence and practice of the gift of tongues as described in Corinth."[6] If we are seeking the power of the Holy Spirit, our attention needs to focus on purity. These comments are not intended to invalidate people's experiences of the gift.

---

[6] Ibid., 13.

A RADIANT CHARACTER

Appendix B

A Model for Small Group Accountability

In Chapter 11 there were comments to encourage everyone, if possible, to be part of a small group as a significant help to holiness. Below is the model that greatly assisted the churches I have served over the last 25 years, (with various degrees of structuring). To repeat what I said then: I am not saying that this model is the *only* possibility. No doubt there are others better qualified and experienced who have developed alternative ones. However, this worked and did provide a framework for ongoing personal growth for those who took it seriously. At the heart of the idea is a commitment to protecting people from unnecessary hurt, and helping them grow.

There are five features of this model:

1) The appointment of a Growth Groups Coordinator to give general ministry oversight of all groups in the church and to minister pastorally, if necessary, to the Growth Group leaders.

2) A focus on accountability with suggested questions to strengthen the focus.

3) The use of a covenant, making expectations clear—not just 'drift and assume'.

4) The *appointment* of people to groups after an interview with the coordinator, rather than just leave them to put their names on a list on the wall at the beginning of the year (as so often happens).

5) There was a high level of freedom in choice of study material to be used (in consultation with the coordinator). Some groups used more advanced study notes but groups made up of new Christians went for more basic ones. That flexibility is important.

Growth Groups are not a substitute for the Holy Spirit's working in our lives. They are like a skeleton to a body—a vital framework. It is a structure through which God can work to enable us to safely help each other change and grow, in obedience to James 5:16, "Confess your sins to each other and pray for each other so that you may be healed" (NLT).

So, what do I mean when I speak of a Growth Group, and how do they work in a local church?

- *Growth Groups* are small groups with a maximum of 12 members.

- *Cell Groups* are same-sex groups of 3 or 4 (maximum) within a Growth Group to assist in-depth sharing, making it safer to share, and cope with time limitations.

- *Care Circles* are those linked with the church but not attending a Growth Group, who have been unofficially allocated to a Growth Group by leadership, for pastoral care and encouragement.

Growth Groups are all about growth—a place where, surrounded by friends, we concentrate on the practical understanding and application of God's Word. Usually there will (and should) be a Bible study component to the meeting, but this is not the primary focus. The group is a place:

- To share the longings of our heart—the things for which we want the prayer support of others.

- Where we can ask others to hold us accountable for following through on a commitment or undertaking. For instance, a change of our attitude in a certain situation; making a difficult phone call, sharing our faith with a friend, keeping our thoughts pure—in other words, applying some truth we have learnt, to our everyday lives. Remember that each member chooses what to share. There is no pressure to do so.

They usually meet weekly in private homes.[1] There can be daytime groups, evening groups, ladies' groups, men's groups, young adult groups, mixed groups—meeting in various suburbs.

Members commit themselves to one another by means of a covenant to keep it a safe place.

---

[1] I have been impressed with some in the USA who meet in McDonalds or similar venue for their men's group. Their very presence and observable friendship dynamic is a testimony and creates opportunities for sharing the faith.

Unlike a contract as we use the word today, the Bible sees a covenant primarily as an agreement surrounded by grace. At its core is the idea of shared relationships along with intention and hope both for listening to each other and for encouragement and support. Below is the one we used:

Growth Group covenant

As a Christian, I desire to become a better disciple of Christ in such areas as worship, outreach, prayer, relationships and intensifying my passion for truth. I realise this cannot happen in isolation so for the next three months I will commit myself to the following disciplines for the purpose of my spiritual growth, the spiritual growth of the group and for the furthering of God's Kingdom.

Attendance:
I will give priority to the group meetings. I will be present and on time, except for emergencies. If I am unable to attend, or if I am unavoidably delayed I will call the group leader to apologise before the meeting starts.

Sharing:
I will share myself as openly as I can and contribute whenever possible so that the group can become a spiritual community. I will go out of my way to welcome newcomers to the group.

Accountability:
I will make myself discreetly accountable to the other members of the cell so that I may become the type of person God wants me to be.

Confidentiality:
I will not discuss anything shared within the group with any person who was not present at the time it was shared. The purpose of this safeguard is to avoid gossip and/or criticism of others in their absence and to protect personal data.

Support:
I will give my best to help the group reach the goals we set together as part of our pursuit of holiness, Christian community and spiritual awakening.

Loyalty:
I will be a loyal and true friend to the members of the group as we seek to grow in our discipleship (1 Corinthians 13). I will uphold

fellow members of the cell regularly in prayer. I will participate regularly in the ministry of this local Church and with God's help I will be a regular, faithful, caring member of the group.

After attending an orientation meeting (or interview) and considering the challenge, opportunity and commitments I feel unworthy, yet challenged to attempt what is asked. I have prayed about these commitments and feel God is leading me to become a Growth Group member.

Signature: _____ (or initials)

Please feel free to reproduce or to adapt the Growth Group Covenant above for use in your group. No copyright permission is required.

Why is a covenant helpful?

If participants are to have security based on trust they need to know what to expect. Having had the opportunity to consider and agree to a standard of behaviour, members can feel safe in their relationships with one another. That is why the initial commitment is for three months. People can, of course, withdraw at any time but an agreed period allows them to re-evaluate their progress, and decide if they wish to continue.

Because sharing will sometimes touch on hurts from others, we found it helpful to add a comment regarding gossip. Great care needs to be taken, as there is a fine line between sharing and gossip. When considering what to share, we need to beware of using the cloak of confidentiality as a cover for gossip or the 'bad-mouthing' of others. The tone of the sharing in a Growth Group should always be positive and God-honouring.

Remember, discussing something with someone who is not part of the problem or part of the answer, is gossip. If we have something against someone, we need to go see *them*—not 'run them down' to others (Matthew 18:15–17). Sharing details of prayer points is an area for special guardedness in this regard.

This caution is necessary because I have come across folk whose groups were going well until someone violated this biblical principle. People were hurt, and so they were reluctant to be part of such a group again. Quitting was not the answer. People involved in a road accident do not quit travelling in cars, although they will probably be more careful next time.

The structure includes

- A *covenant* setting out expectations
- Support for the Growth Group leader by the person coordinating the ministry
- Job Description to ensure quality
- Appointment methods including an interview with the Growth Group Coordinator to hear the person's thoughts on such questions as:
  1) Whom would you like to be with?
  2) Whom would you *not* like to be with?
  3) Is there a particular time that suits?
  4) Is there a location you would like?
  5) Would you like to link it with a particular ministry team you are in?[2]

After the interview, a group can be suggested but it may be for a trial time to see if the person feels they fit. This method takes account of the fact that some will not join a group because they need to feel safe to share freely in their group, and we want as many as possible to benefit from the Groups.

There have been several times in different churches when someone has made a comment to me such as, "I notice that ...... has put his/her name down for our group next year. I feel uncomfortable with them so I'll just say, 'I'm not well' for the first few meetings then no one will miss me." When I hear such a remark, I am saddened because poor practice is damaging that person—or at the very least hindering them from having safe access to help.

Years ago, I read a quote from John Powell: "Why am I afraid to tell you who I am? Because you might not like who I am and it's all I've got!" We all need a safe place to be transparent and still be loved.

Answers to frequently asked questions

1. Can a person who does not regularly attend this local church be a member of a Growth Group?

---

[2] Some groups link their sharing with a team ministry such as music practice, and the occasion includes time for both but avoids the need for a second trip out at another time in the week.

Members are encouraged to invite newcomers to Growth Groups after consultation with the group leader. A Growth Group is a safe place for a seeker to learn about Jesus and to experience first-hand the love and grace of a genuine Christian community. I like the term 'port of entry'.

2. What if I have nothing to share with the others in my cell?

Being in a Growth Group does not mean that you need to have lots of problems to share with others. If everything is going well for you, then you have much for which to praise God. You can share this with the group. Maybe you can encourage others by sharing a 'gem' that you read or heard. It is more difficult if you do not feel able to share the things that are really troubling you. You might be able to share at some level and ask them to pray for the deeper problem without going into details. It might be helpful to talk with your Growth Group leader, pastor or another trusted counsellor.

3. What happens if a confidence is broken?

Your Growth Group leader should be told immediately and the matter may be referred to one of the pastors. The person responsible needs to be lovingly confronted about the broken confidence so things can be made right with you and future participation is safe.

4. What if I can't be there every week?

Some people will have great difficulty making a commitment to a weekly meeting. Shift work, for instance, can make regular attendance difficult. If you are nevertheless committed to participation in a Growth Group, plan to be there as often as you can. When you can't attend, phone and apologise. You can let the leader know how you are going and perhaps send a message to the rest of the group about a particular need, or praise point. Try to keep in contact with other members of your group during the week. Beware of letting your irregular attendance become an easy excuse. Make sure you do attend all the meetings you can.

5. What happens when our group grows too big?

Growth Groups are designed to grow. Numerical growth is a healthy sign—we are not only stretched by accepting and welcoming newcomers but our lives are greatly enriched. When the group has twelve members it is time to 'birth' a second group—and that is exciting!!! If the host and leader are two different people, part of the group goes with each and continuity is not lost.

6. What if I want to change groups or leave the group?

Leaving your Growth Group should be a conscious decision. You should think and pray about it and be sure of God's leading. Just drifting out of the group is bad for you and bad for the group. If you feel you should change groups or leave, consult your Growth Group Coordinator or the pastor. If possible, let the group leader know of your plans. Your group will miss you. Leaving the group should be a positive, not a negative step.

7. If God leads me to be part of another church, can I remain in a Growth Group of this local church?

Unfortunately, the answer is "no". Growth Groups are not isolated units that stand-alone. They are part of the ministry of the local church. It is important for members of a Growth Group to share the vision and goals of that local church, so that they move forward as a complete unit. The Growth Group leader is in fact an extension of the pastor's ministry. Part of the Covenant agreed to, is *loyalty* not only to each other but to this local church. By becoming part of another church, you have in effect also resigned from your Growth Group. If God has called you to be part of another church, you need to give your whole-hearted support to this new step in your journey and not be looking back over your shoulder at what you have left behind. We will be sad to say goodbye but will pray that God will help you settle in quickly to your new church and become a part of the small-group life there.

My experience has *consistently* shown that when departing Christians try to stay in the small group to which they have belonged, people are seriously damaged because of a divided loyalty. This applies both to those trying to 'sit on the fence', and to their friends.

Why is structure important?

An emphasis on a fully devoted, godly lifestyle is one of the distinctives of the Christian church. This has been the key to the great revivals of the past. There is weighty evidence that it was the small groups of this kind in the 18th and 19th centuries that allowed God's blessing in sending revival to continue and to reach new people. Thankfully it is being rediscovered in our day.

As God works in our lives, the mutual support and accountability of a Growth Group help to translate our personal experience of full devotion and a disciplined life into action. This is the key to change for our society.

Since the word *accountability* has been used several times it is important to explain what I mean by it. It is 'helping people keep *their* commitments to God'. I learned early in small groups that when I shared a challenge I was facing, and asked the other men to question me next week, it helped me follow through when the pressure came on. I was still the one deciding which area to share and how much. There was no loss of freedom but an extra help to overcome. Some things are not appropriate for the group, and the participants always have the final choice in their comments.

The revival we seek, both personally and nationally, will come only as we apply God's truth to our lives in the context of fellowship with God's people. I mentioned earlier that the 18th century small group which Wesley called a 'class', was a strategic part of consolidating the spiritual awakening of that period. At its heart was the use of accountability questions to help sharpen the focus of sharing and the purpose of personal spiritual development.

There are 'Accountability Questions' below which some groups find helpful. Remember it is only a sample, but take time to think how it could help with accountability.

Another essential facet of this model is that it is vital for leaders to be trained and to meet regularly usually with the pastor and Growth Group Coordinator. This is important not just for feed-back to the church leadership but it nourishes the sense of calling for the group leader as such a role clearly includes a pastoral component. Please remember that the whole accountability idea is counter to our undisciplined culture, and so the leaders will need extra encouragement. Hull has correctly shown that the mentoring (linked with a group) is part of the missing key to the change of character.[3] A quick example is the way the leader protects the sharing time: When a person expresses a challenge they are facing, unfortunately sometimes group members feel it is their duty to begin 'problem solving' on the spot. The leader needs to be aware of this danger and guard against it.

I am indebted to Promise Keepers for ideas which helped prepare the following questions. In all groups, the person chose one area he was concentrating on. No one was ever expected to go over all of

---

[3] Hull, *Choose the Life*, 36–37.

them each week. This model is more like the 'band' and 'select societies' that Wesley and his friends used with success.

Accountability questions

1) Money:

   In the past week, have any of my financial dealings lacked integrity? Have I been faithful in my tithes and giving this week?

2) Sex:

   In the past week, have I been with a member of the opposite sex in a compromising situation? Have I exposed myself to inappropriate sexually explicit material?

3) *Power*:

   In the past week, have I treated others with the dignity and respect that is due to them because of who they are in the eyes of God? Have I attempted to take advantage of or manipulate others?

4) *Attitude*:

   Have I harboured attitudes of bitterness, jealousy, or unforgiveness towards others?

5) Spiritual Walk:

   In the past week, have I achieved my goals in daily devotional time with God? What passages of scripture have been highlights in the past week? Have I read scripture with a heart and a mind open to what God has to say to me? What spiritual truths have I discovered?

6) *Church*:

   In the past week, have I been faithful to the ministry God has called me to? Have I actively supported and prayed for my church and pastors?

7) *Family*:

   In the past week, have I spent quality time with and given priority to my family and my spouse?

8) *Work*:

   In the past week, have I been faithful to my calling at work? Did I shine for Jesus in my workplace?

9) *Physical*:
   In the past week, have I taken care of the body God has given me?

10) *Outreach*:
    In the past week, have I been alert to and responded to opportunities to reach others for Jesus?

11) Question for the Participant:

Which of the foregoing areas am I working on at this time? In what area do I want my cell group to pray for me?

This appendix has focused on the big picture of the model which served the groups, but a special resource for leaders is available if you email the author at hardgrave@protonmail.com. It includes position descriptions and more detail, but please do not try to set up such a ministry in a local church without the full support and permission of the pastor.

Appendix C

A Sample Daily Affirmation

The following are quotes which I have adapted (and some of my own short summary sentences) that are part of my Daily Affirmation. They help sustain me. I have gathered or composed them over the years and I encourage you to do similarly.

The dream in the heart of God for my world in my lifetime is a mighty spiritual awakening. *He* is the Lord of history. I am ..... [*insert your name*] ..... Again today, I identify with His dream and accept it as my life's purpose.

I thank You that no matter what I feel or experience, You have allowed it. I give the issue to You and focus on You. Help me to love You more.

My talents, gifts, experience and personality are all linked with Your plan for my life, and You will bring them together in the right time and way—I'm working not just *for* You, but *with* You as You live in me.

Discipleship will remain my priority as it is Your last command and my first concern.

If I don't like something, I must change it, or my attitude. What I used to call problems are in fact simply challenges to help my faith grow.

We are sending a different kind of person into the community to change it. Please bless me and expand my influence, that Your Hand would be with me in all I do, and keep me from evil, or causing pain.[1]

Please open the door to the right work that will enable me to make my finest contribution to Your kingdom. He Who began a good work in me will complete it until the day of Jesus Christ.[2]

---

[1] Based on 1 Chronicles 4:10. Prayer of Jabez.

When foundations are shaken, doors fly open unexpectedly. Just think of Philippi (Acts 16). That earthquake is a picture of our world today, and new doors are opening as never before.

I will be glad for all God is planning for me.[3]

..... [Add here scriptures that are special to you] .....

The sayings in Chapter 10 were to give you the idea. You could include any of those (or others). Here are a couple more you may enjoy:

Yesterday ended last night, and the future is as bright as the promises of God.[4]

Faith cannot co-exist with certainty. Without an element of mystery and doubt, it isn't faith!

In order to say 'Yes' to God and His dream for my life, I will sometimes have to say 'No' in this day, often to requests for worthy causes. When I do, it will be because of the intensity burning within me of my passionate 'Yes' to Him and His call on my life.

The next one is a favourite which has helped me cope with life's betrayals and disappointments, and I always end my Affirmation with it:

That is why the sons and daughters of Wesley live with a sparkle in their eye. The church militant will become the church triumphant. Why should we care where God places us in His service? That is His affair, not ours. And whatever our appointed work, we know that nothing can ultimately prevail against Immanuel's mission.[5]

[2] Based on Philippians 1:6
[3] Based on Romans 12:12
[4] Kingsley Ridgway speaking in Maryborough, Queensland in 1978.
[5] Robert E. Coleman, *Nothing to do but to Save Souls* (Grand Rapids, MI: Francis Asbury Press, 1990), 101.

Appendix D

Questions for Reflection or Discussion

Before you read each chapter ask God to focus your mind on His word to you from this material and to reveal Himself to you afresh.

Have your pen and journal handy to be able to jot down insights or ideas that come to you.

Do not share personal data with a small group unless it is protected by a covenant of confidentiality.

If the questions are for a group, the leader may say which ones will be the focus of 'next week'.

Those marked with an asterisk are for private reflection but a group may like to use them.

Chapter 1: The need for a radiant character

1) Do you agree with the quote in the introduction that "Every normal person would like to be a radiant personality?" Why might this be so?
2) Do you think it is true that the starting place for rebuilding our nation must be with the kind of people who make up the church?
3) If you were talking to an unchurched person about prayer how would you describe it?
4) Reflect on what you believe about the idea of moving beyond conversion to a 'higher plane', and whether it really makes a difference?
5) Are your beliefs built on the truth-foundation of scripture? Why is that important?
6) *Are you content to settle for mediocre Christianity or do you desire to be 'totally sold out' for Christ?
7) When you conclude this time, share the prayer for our nation that God will 'bend down to the dying embers of a fire just about to go out, breathing into it until it bursts into flame'.

Chapter 2: What does it mean to be a follower of Christ?

1) Why do so many Christians have so few unchurched friends?
2) How might this hinder the spread of the gospel?
3) Recall when you first made a decision to accept Jesus as your Lord and Saviour. Reflect on your journey so far. What memories stand out for you? Can you see a pattern of growth like the disciples?
4) Jacob's life describes a contrast between Bethel and Peniel. Is that contrast common today?
5) What characteristics caught your attention from the lives described in the second part of Chapter 2?
6) Is there one of the people described about whom you would like to learn more?
7) What application of the truths do you want to make in your life?
8) *Reflect on Archbishop Fenelon's understanding of the holy life as six steps.

Chapter 3: Testimonies—more than 'fire insurance'

1) Did the magnet illustration and application sound 'true to life' to you?
2) Identify in which areas you are growing and learning and which areas need to be worked on.
3) Think about the idea of a moment of crisis or full commitment which was preceded and followed by growth in godliness and love for God, plus a passion for the truths of scripture. Does this sound true to you?
4) Did you recognize that each person had a varied journey? Is that important in your thinking?
5) Take a moment to reread Francis Ridley Havergal's note to her sister "First I was shown..."
6) *Are you daily totally yielded and utterly trusting Jesus?
7) Which testimonies challenged you the most? Plan to research more into their lives.

Chapter 4: The heart of the problem—our inner civil war

1) Consider the account of the prisoner-of-war camp as one of the women watched a Nazi guard beating her friend. Is there a danger that we tend to ignore?
2) *Read Romans 6:12–13 remembering the commands which indicate our responsibility as a Christian. Make a note in your journal about this. If you have time read James 4:7 and 2 Peter 3:14.
3) Reread 1 Corinthians 10:13 and reflect on a time when you have been tempted, but God had made a way of escape or removal from a situation. Take time to thank God and pray.
4) Are there any areas in your life that need to be 'nourished' by more of the following: studying or reading the Bible, fellowship, worshiping with others or areas which you may need to be 'starved' of: ungodly internet sites, movies, songs, just wasted time surfing the net, etc.?
5) Our society is busy. How easy is it to just drift rather than taking steps to change?
6) *Reflect on the paragraph about repentance, full consecration, acceptance by faith. Be honest with yourself and ask God to reveal areas for further growth.
7) Every church has an atmosphere. What do you think visitors sense when they visit your church? How could it be enhanced?

Chapter 5: What is repentance and why does it matter?

1) In your own words explain repentance and why it matters.
2) How is it different from remorse?
3) Were you surprised by the material on pride? Do you agree that it 'always means submerged (and often disguised) antagonism and rivalry'? Ask God to bring anything to the surface for you to deal with and repent of.
4) Do you agree with White's words 'the earthquake of repentance is the doorway to faith and behavioural change? It's the beginning of true enlightenment?'
5) *Ask God to reveal any areas of your life you need to bring before the cross—one by one—and seek repentance, forgiveness, healing, freedom. Is there one area you would like your friends to pray for you to have God's help?
6) Why do you think the artist repairing the Pieta had to study Michelangelo's life? Any lessons for us?

Chapter 6: The teaching of the Bible about a godly life

1) How important is the distinction between 'blameless' and 'faultless'?
2) 'It would be absurd for God to expect us to confess something we do not know is wrong'. Do you agree? Why?
3) Did the promise of a pure heart in this life give you hope?
4) *Reflect on the saying 'as I look back, this is what matters; I have loved and been loved, all the rest is background music'. Is this true for you? What might you need to change?
5) Paul's prayer for the Thessalonian Christians (5:23–24) has much to teach us. What stands out to you as you think about the various parts.
6) What do you think is the most important difference between the old and new covenants?
7) The last paragraph notes the words of Dr Sangster's friend "this will do you no good unless you take it".
8) *Write a list of things to follow through and implement—those that you have been challenged by—unintentional sins, movies, purity of heart, abiding in love.
9) Do you think it would help if a safe close friend held you accountable?

Chapter 7: An expanded horizon—moving to maturity

1) Are the steps to being filled with the Holy Spirit relevant to today's Christians?
2) Consider the thought that there is usually a delay between conversion and this deeper work. Is it helpful in understanding our journey?
3) What is the difference between temptation and sin?
4) Reread the paragraph 'A thought on forgiveness' and the comment— "If God can forgive us, we can also stop blaming ourselves." Why do we tend to do this?
5) *Write out at least one of the Bible promises you can claim on card/paper, place it somewhere prominent and memorize this scripture passage, to recall and declare in times of trial.
6) *Reflect on Leonardo's insight and ask God to reveal any unforgiveness in your heart.
7) *Reflect on the seven points under the heading 'In a nutshell' on being filled with the Holy Spirit.

Chapter 8: Total commitment

1) How well do you handle unanswered prayer? Forgiveness?
2) What 'good intentions' did you have in the past month which you did not act on?
3) Reflect on Luke 11:9: "So I say to you, ask and it will be given to you; seek and you will find; knock and it will be opened to you."' Read verses 1–13 to see the verses in context. Write out your own reflective prayer or you may like to start with the one in this book. Remember to praise and thank God for answers.
4) Write or print Philippians 4:8 on card and have it in your prayer journal as a reflective pruning/refining process in your prayer life. Ask the questions honestly: true, honest, just, pure, lovely, of good report, excellent and praiseworthy.
5) *Reflect on David Seamands' idea that the aim of God in self surrender is not the destruction of self, it is the birth and the growth of the true self He intended you to be.
6) Do you have a clear vision of God's calling on your life?
7) *Further reflect on Seamands comments on self-surrender and ask God to reveal any parts of your life you have been holding back.
8) Check your music library. What are you listening to? Is there any change required?
9) Ephesians 5:20 "giving thanks always for all things," is this your daily 'faith response' for all that happens. Be encouraged to bring faith to bear and affirm the sovereignty of God, believing for the blessing not yet seen.

Chapter 9: A disciplined routine

1) Do you have as part of your regular routine a Quiet Time to meet with the Lord—a divine appointment with your best Friend?
2) What are the benefits for having the same place each day?
3) What does it mean to meditate on scripture as in Joshua 1:8?
4) Refer to the 'helpful questions' we can ask ourselves and the additional three tests in the paragraph titled 'Convictions in Specific Areas' and honestly relate these to specific areas of your life and choices you are currently making.
5) Do you have a devotions framework like A.C.T.S. and are you journaling what God is teaching or revealing to you? Which one of the four are you most likely to omit?
6) *What things are most likely to hinder your praying?

7) Does writing out your prayers help or hinder your prayer?
8) Did Brother Lawrence's idea of practising the presence of God sound challenging to you?

Chapter 10: A guarded imagination

1) What ways have you found to use imagination in your praying?
2) How useful is journalling for you?
3) *Take time to reread Appendix C 'A Sample Daily Affirmation' and start the process of producing your own personal daily affirmation. Remember to: make it personal, looking to tomorrow, with a capacity to inspire.
4) How much of a challenge is the pressure of technology on your time budget?
5) When tempted, is 'thought displacement' any help in your world?
6) Reflect on Victor Frankl's saying for which he became famous 'the last of the great human freedoms is the freedom to choose one's attitude in any given set of circumstances'. Have you had situations over which you felt you had no control over, but were able to choose to control your reactions.
7) Reread scriptures: Romans 12:2, 2 Corinthians 10:5, Philippians 4:8 and the 'I can' list from Paul's letter, be challenged to daily responding as scripture leads you.
8) Take a moment to ask God to reveal firstly hurts received from others and forgive them and then secondly hurts committed against God. Make a list. Pray through the items extending and seeking forgiveness and then, as though cancelling an invoice, write diagonally Matthew 6:14 on hurts against yourself and 1 John 1:9 on hurts against God. Then burn the list after prayer and 'watch it burn'(—obviously in a place where there is no fire risk).

Chapter 11: Accountability—supported by friends

1) Reflecting on Jesus example of time with his disciples—the small group that provided a perfect learning environment. Do you agree with the value of accountability and learning in a small group?

2) In what situations are you already held accountable—traffic violation, taxes?

3) Can you think of two roles in our society where we wish people were more accountable?

4) Are you currently in a small group? If not pray for guidance on which group to join.

5) *Have you been in a small group and felt betrayed/hurt by a well-meaning person? Check your response and whether there has been forgiveness or is this holding you back from attending, committing and sharing.

6) Has your small group discussed a covenant that you have all agreed to? Have a look at the suggested covenant listing: attendance, sharing, accountability, confidentiality, support, loyalty.

7) Reflect on the comment about 'gossip' and be mindful of the warning: 'Discussing something with someone who is not part of the problem or part of the answer, is gossip. If we have something against someone we need to go see them, not 'run them down' to others' (Matthew 18:15-17). Why is special care needed with prayer requests?

8) Review the accountability questions and being mindful of these, share with a trusted friend and ask them to pray with and hold you accountable. (Start with one area.)

Chapter 12: Investing in others

1) How do we define success? How do we decide if we have achieved it?

2) In what areas of your life would you like to see changes? What barriers hinder that process?

3) The feeling that we are facing life's problems in isolation from others can contribute to loneliness. How can we help minimize that?

4) *Reflect on the following questions as you choose the higher way, to be filled and controlled by the Holy Spirit and to discover God's plan and destiny for your life.

   a) Have you made a total commitment realizing there will be a cost?

b) What will you do with the insights gleaned?

c) Do you know who you are and what you are doing here?

5) What things are most likely to improve your relationships with others you care about?

6) Do you feel well prepared to answer the following questions on judgement day?

  a) What have you done about the wrong things of which you are guilty? (That is about salvation.)

  b) What have you done with the gifts and opportunities you were given? (That is about stewardship.)

  c) Whom have you brought with you? (That is about sharing our faith.)

7) What do you think of the quote 'true freedom is not to be found in the absence of slavery but in the service of a wonderful master'?

Bibliography

Agnew, Milton S. *Transformed Christians—New Testament Messages on Holy Living.* Kansas City, MO: Beacon Hill Press of Kansas City, 1974.

Backus, William. *Finding the Freedom of Self-Control.* Minneapolis, MN: Bethany House Publishers, 1987.

Backus, William and Chapian, Marie. *Why Do I Do What I Don't Want to Do?* Minneapolis, MN: Bethany House Publishers, 1984.

Brengle, S. L. *Heart Talks on Holiness.* Salvationist Publishing and Supplies Ltd. "https://jesus.org.uk/sites/default/files/media/documents/.../heart-talks-on-holiness.pdf".

_____. *Helps to Holiness.* https://jesus.org.uk/sites/default/files/media/documents/books/.../helps-to-holiness.pdf".

_____. *When the Holy Ghost is Come.* New York: Cosimo Classics, 2005.

Bridges, Jerry. *The Pursuit of Holiness.* Colorado Springs, CA: NavPress, 1978.

Bright, Bill. *How to Walk in the Spirit—Transferable Concept 4.* Campus Crusade for Christ, Inc., 1971.

_____. *The Coming Revival.* Orlando FL: NewLife publications—Campus Crusade for Christ, 1995.

Cameron, Lindsay. *Methodism Reborn—The Wesleyan Methodist Church in the South Pacific.* Perth, Australia: Cypress Project, 2017.

Clark, Glenn. *I Will Lift Up Mine Eyes.* The Drift, Evesham, Worcs: Arthur James Limited, 1953.

Coleman, Robert E. *"Nothing to Do but to Save Souls"—John Wesley's Charge to His Preachers.* Grand Rapids, MI: Francis Asbury Press, 1990.

_____. *The Master Plan of Evangelism.* Old Tappan, NJ: Fleming H. Revell Company, 2nd Edition, 1964.

Cook, Thomas. *New Testament Holiness.* Fort Washington, PA: Christian Literature Crusade, n.d.

Crabb, Larry. *The Safest Place on Earth—Where People Connect and Are Forever Changed.* Nashville, TN: W Publishing Group a division of Thomas Nelson, 1999.

Deck, R. (Hymn writer). *The Keswick Hymn Book,* "I Take Thy promise, Lord". London: Marshall, Morgan & Scott, Ltd., n.d.), Hymn 107.

175

DeNeff, Steve. *More Than Forgiveness*. Indianapolis, IN: Wesleyan Publishing House, 2002.

_____. *Whatever Became of Holiness?* Indianapolis, IN: Wesleyan Publishing House, 1996.

Drury, Keith. *Disciplines of Holy Living.* Indianapolis, IN: Wesley Press, 1989. (In 2004, reprinted under the title: *Spiritual Disciplines for Ordinary People.*)

_____. (Editor: Holdren, David W.). *Holiness for Ordinary People*. Marion, IN: The Wesley Press, 1983.

_____. *Money, Sex & Spiritual Power*. Indianapolis, IN: Wesley Press, 1992.

Edman, V. Raymond. *They Found the Secret*. London: Marshall, Morgan and Scott, 1st British Edition, 1961.

Foster, Richard J. *Celebration of Discipline—The Path to Spiritual Growth*. London: Hodder and Stoughton, 1980.

_____. *Money, Sex & Power—The Challenge to the Disciplined Life*. London: Hodder and Stoughton, 1985.

Gabriel, Charles Homer. (Hymn writer). *The Methodist Hymnbook*, "He Lifted Me". London: Methodist Conference Office, Revised 1954, Hymn 336.

Geiger, Kenneth (Compiler). *Insights into Holiness,* Chapter by Nicholson, Roy S. "Holiness and the Human Element". Kansas City, MO: Beacon Hill Press, 1963.

_____. *Further Insights into Holiness*. Kansas City, MO: Beacon Hill Press, 1963.

Graham, Billy. *World Aflame*. Melbourne: William Heinemann Ltd., Australian Paperback edition, 1967.

Griffiths, Michael C. *Three Men Filled with the Spirit—The Gift of Tongues: Must It Divide Us?* London: Overseas Missionary Fellowship, 1969.

Grubb, Norman P. *The Liberating Secret*. London: Lutterworth Press, 1955.

Hammond, T. C. *In Understanding Be Men*. London: IVF Publishing, fifth edition, 1954.

Hardgrave, Don. *You can Know God's Will*. Macgregor, Qld: A Pleasant Surprise Ltd., 1990.

Harper, Albert F. (General Editor). "*Study Helps*", contained in *The Wesley Bible—New King James Version—A Personal Study Bible for Holy Living*. Nashville: Thomas Nelson Publishers, 1990.

Hegre, T. A. *The Cross and Sanctification*. Minneapolis, MN: Bethany Fellowship, Inc., 1960.

Henderson, D. Michael. *John Wesley's Class Meeting—A Model for Making Disciples.* Nappanee, IN: Francis Asbury Press of Evangel Publishing House, 1997.

Huddleston, Brad. *Digital Cocaine—A Journey Towards iBalance.* Vereeniging 1930 RSA:Christian Art Publishers, 2016.

Hull, Bill. *Building High Commitment in a Low Commitment World.* Grand Rapids, MI: Fleming H. Revell, 1995.

_____. *Choose the Life—Exploring a Faith that Embraces Discipleship.* Grand Rapids, MI: Baker Books, 2004.

_____. *The Disciple Making Pastor—The Key to Building Healthy Christians in Today's Church.* Grand Rapids, MI: Fleming H. Revell, 1997.

Lawson, James Gilchrist. *Deeper Experiences of Famous Christians.* Anderson, IN: The Warner Press, 1911.

Lewis, C. S. *Mere Christianity.* London: Fontana Books, 1954.

Lloyd-Jones, D. Martyn. *Romans—Exposition of Chapter 8:5–17—The Sons of God.* Edinburgh: The Banner of Truth Trust, 1974.

MacDonald, Gordon. *Ordering Your Private World.* Chicago: Moody Press, 1984.

_____. *Rebuilding Your Broken World.* Nashville, TN: Oliver Nelson, a Division of Thomas Nelson Inc., 1st British edition, 1988.

Maltz, Maxwell. *Psycho-Cybernetics.* New York: Pocket Books, 1969.

Maxwell, John C. *Developing the Leader Within You.* Nashville: Thomas Nelson Publishers, 1993.

_____. *Your Attitude: Key to Success.* San Bernadino, CA: Here's Life Publishers Inc., 1984.

McDowell Josh. *His Image, My Image—Biblical Principles for Improving Your Self-Image.* San Bernardino, CA: Here's Life Publishers, Inc. (A Campus Crusade for Christ Book),1984.

McGrath, Alister E. *The Future of Christianity.* Oxford, UK: Blackwell Publishers Ltd., 2002.

Micklethwait, John and Wooldridge, Adrian. *God is Back—How the Global Rise of Faith Is Changing the World.* Great Britain: Allen Lane, 2009.

Morgan, G. Campbell. *Discipleship.* London: Morgan and Scott Ltd.,1897.

Murray, Iain H. *Australian Christian Life From 1788—An Introduction and an Anthology.* Edinburgh: The Banner of Truth Trust, 1988.

Nee, Watchman. *The Normal Christian Life.* London and Eastbourne: Victory Press, 1969.

Peale, Norman Vincent. *The Positive Power of Jesus Christ.* London: Hodder and Stoughton, 1981.

Piggin, Stuart. *Firestorm of the Lord—The History of and Prospects for Revival in the Church and the World.* Cumbria UK: Paternoster Press, 2000.

_____. *Spirit of a Nation—The Story of Australia's Christian Heritage.* Sydney: Strand Publishing, 2004.

Purkiser, W. T., et al. *God, Man, & Salvation.* Kansas City, MI: Beacon Hill Press of Kansas City, 1977.

Redpath, Alan. *Victorious Christian Living—Studies in the Book of Joshua.* Basingstoke, Hants, UK: Pickering & Inglis, 1st British edition, 1956.

Ridgway, Kingsley M. *In Search of God—An Account of Ministerial Labours in Australia and the Islands of the Sea*, 1937. Republished in *Pioneer with a Passion,* 2nd edition, ed. Lindsay Cameron. Australia: Wesleyan Methodist Church, 2011.

Robinson, Martin. *To Win the West.* Crowborough, East Sussex: Monarch Publications,1996.

Sangster, W. E. *The Path to Perfection.* London: Hodder and Stoughton,1943.

_____. *The Pure in Heart.* London: The Epworth Press, 1954.

_____. *The Secret of Radiant Life.* London: Hodder and Stoughton, 2nd Edition, 1963.

Schuller, Robert. H. *Move Ahead with Possibility Thinking.* Garden City, N.Y.: Doubleday and Company, Inc., 1967.

Seamands, David A. *Putting Away Childish Things—Reprogram Old Behaviour Patterns That are Holding You Back.* Wheaton, IL: Victor Books, 1982.

Stott, John. *The Radical Disciple—Wholehearted Christian Living.* Nottingham: Inter-Varsity Press, 2010.

Taylor, Richard S. *A Right Conception of Sin.* Kansas City: Beacon Hill Press, 1945.

Turner, George Allen. *The Vision Which Transforms.* Kansas City, MO: Beacon Hill Press,1964.

Tuttle, Robert G. Jr. *John Wesley: His Life and Theology.* Grand Rapids: Zondervan Publishing House,1978.

Vine, W. E. *An Expository Dictionary of New Testament Words.* Old Tappan, NJ: Fleming H. Revell Company, 1940.

Wall, Phil. *"I'll Fight... Holiness at War".* Kent, England: Sovereign World Ltd., 1998.

White, John. *Changing on the Inside—The Keys to Spiritual Recovery and Lasting Change.* Guilford, Surrey: Eagle, 1991.

Wood, A. Skevington. *The Burning Heart.* London: The Paternoster Press, 1967.

Wright, Tom. *Virtue Reborn.* London: SPCK, 2010.

Yancey, Philip. *Praying with the KGB—A Startling Report from a Shattered Empire.* Portland, OR: Multnomah Press, 1992.

_____. *What's So Amazing About Grace?* Grand Rapids, MI: Zondervan Publishing House, 1997.

Other Sources:

Zacharias, Ravi. DVD: *Is There Meaning in Evil and Suffering?* Presented by the Faith and Science Lecture Forum in Atlanta GA.

Endorsements

You will love this book. And the book will prompt you to love Christ more. Here is a practical guide to entering the life of holiness which is eminently practical while at the same time being a solid researched work suitable for the classroom. Here, Don Hardgrave collects together the testimonies of Christians past and present who have experienced a deeper walk with God—a walk of holiness in heart and lifestyle leading to a "radiant life." Here you will find the Bible and theology undergirding the holy life plus practical help for entering and living such a life. The book is written so clearly it sounds like Don Hardgrave himself is sitting with the reader having a pastoral chat. I hope thousands will read this book and understand and enter "the radiant life. "

Keith Drury, Professor Emeritus,
Indiana Wesleyan University, USA.
Author, *Holiness for Ordinary people.*

The book, *How to Be a Radiant Character*, by author Dr Don Hardgrave provides a valuable guide for individuals, churches and the extended Christian community in grasping a Biblically based theology of Christian experience. Written from a Wesleyan Arminian theological perspective, Dr Hardgrave systematically builds a thorough and clear explanation of the attainable and expected realities of spiritual life. The potential of a radiant character comes by grace from God, the Father, through the work of Jesus Christ and made real through the enabling power and presence of the Holy Spirit. The author builds this truth through a masterful linkage and application of an amazing number of scriptural passages. A radiant character is scripturally possible. Therefore, it is a Biblical mandate for each Christian to experience.

Dr Hardgrave uses a variety of Biblical translations to present his message. This strengthens his presentation. Further, he draws upon quotes of many voices of past, notable church leaders and interweaves the observations and testimonies of many contemporary Christian leaders as well. This book abounds in practical application of Biblical truth in real life situations. He interweaves numerous illustrations that confirm the validity of his analysis—often with a delightful, humorous point. The reader comes to a conclusion that what Dr Hardgrave presents is truth, Biblical truth, liveable truth possible for and expected of each Christian. The entire Christian community, whether on a personal basis, or in a small group study setting or from the pulpit in public proclamation, will benefit from the thoughtful, thorough explanation of a radiant character as a norm of Christian experience.

Dr Daniel L. Tipton, Past General Superintendent,
Churches of Christ in Christian Union, USA.

A smooth read—a challenging journey—an innovative look at the work of the Spirit in producing and sustaining holiness and therefore radiance. It is all of grace, yet personal effort plays its part. The greatest part of that effort is in constantly handing over our will to the indwelling Spirit who in turn takes over directing our new-born spirit to instruct our mind and body and thus carry out His purpose for our lives—to achieve a radiant destiny.

Dr Stan Solomon, Past General Superintendent,
Baptist Union, QLD, Australia.

I have had the privilege of knowing Rev. Dr Don Hardgrave for over 40 years, as my pastor, my previous District and National Superintendent, and as a friend. I remember a young Vietnamese lady, by the name of Lien Nguyen, who said after her first encounter with Don's preaching, "for the first time I have had many of my questions about God and faith answered, and I want to keep coming to find out more". That was over 35 years ago and now that lady has been my wife for 32 years. I guess I have a lot to thank Don for.

Many people like my wife and I have been impacted by Don's ministry over many decades. From day one within the Wesleyan Methodist Church, God has used Don to turn a church into a movement, from a flickering flame to a growing National Church. Under his leadership and personal involvement, 31 churches were planted in 15 years in Queensland, in addition to churches in other states.

One of Don's key emphases has been the development of the youth camping movement that has transformed the lives of many of our youth, who like me are now in leadership within the church. Other key aspects of his ministry have been his commitment to the exposition of biblical principles that enable local churches to exercise faith, make disciples, build leaders and shape effective small groups. While some have found it hard to keep up with Don's pace, because of his incredible energy and discipline, one cannot help but be impacted by his passion. One of his messages that still rings in my ear today is "How high is your desperation level?", like so many of his other messages that move you into action with a passion for a lost and dying world.

It is out of a wealth of knowledge, a depth of research, and years of fruitful experience that Don has compiled this resource. It is a challenge for the Christian who is longing for so much more. The deeper life is a topic dear to my heart. There is no doubt that there is a lack of Biblical understanding today within the church around the subject of the deeper life. This book is both inspirational and transformational. It goes a long way towards clearing the haze around the possibility and process of living such a life. I would encourage readers to dive into its pages with the desire to be and have all that God intended for you.

Rev. Rex E Rigby, South QLD and National Superintendent,
South Pacific Regional Conference President
Wesleyan Methodist Church of Australia.

'Radiant' may not be a popular word today but undoubtedly all serious followers of Jesus aspire to have an authentic testimony growing to be more like Jesus as they learn to keep in step with the Holy Spirit. The author not only describes the radiant life but gives many practical examples of how we may attain it. Each concept is clearly explained and illustrated with stories from history as well as from the author's own experience. Don Hardgrave explains clearly that, while it is the work of the Holy Spirit to bring about change, we have a definite role in the process through living a disciplined life. I believe the apostle Paul summarises this balance in living the Christian life when in explaining his aim to present everyone mature in Christ, he says, "To this end I labour, struggling with all his energy, which so powerfully works in me." Col 1:29

A great feature of this book is the suggested discussion questions included for each chapter. This makes the book an ideal resource for small groups.

Keith Cruickshank, Past Principal,
GLO Training Centre, TAS, Australia.

Don Hardgrave's passion for a vital relationship with Jesus Christ is expressed through the pages of this book. Years of effective ministry and reflection in a variety of contexts gives Hardgrave a refreshingly practical perspective on being a disciple of Christ. His frequent reference to Scripture, and his recording of personal anecdotes, reveals a profound commitment to authentic Christian living that the reader will find challenging and inspiring.

Dr Bruce Allder, Past Principal,
Nazarene Training College, Australia.

Is it possible to live our lives in which Jesus has the prominent place? There are many books which speak of the pursuit of holiness, some of which are now considered Christian 'classics'. So why do we need another one? Don Hardgrave provides a manual for holiness with a refreshing Australian accent! He has the 'runs on the board' and brings the result of many years of Bible study, teaching and leading young followers of Jesus. Don walks faithfully with Jesus and genuinely desires to bring others along in that walk. Using strong Biblical foundations, this book provides clear and practical instruction for the 21st century follower of Jesus.

Rev. Bob Rogers, Director of Field Education,
Brisbane School of Theology, QLD, Australia.

The Apostle Paul could have written the sub title to this book; '... keep in step with the Spirit.' (Galatians 5:25 (see 22-26). In this 500th year since Luther nailed his 95 Thesis to the castle church door, Don Hardgrave has nailed his 12 chapters to our interdenominational church doors. Our culture has descended into a new dark age and tragically many Christian believers are living in the shadows. This book draws believers back into gospel light and living. While not everyone will agree with everything Don has written (and that's healthy), it is a testimony to Jesus' grand statement 'I will build my church (Matthew 16:18). Don wears his Wesleyan heart on his sleeve— to the benefit and up building of us all. This book should be read across denominational lines because the issue is that the best days of the church are yet to come! Therefore, let's keep in step with the Spirit.

Rev. Greg Fraser,
Presbyterian Church, Stanthorpe, QLD, Australia.

Dr Don Hardgrave writes with all the authority of an evangelical leader that has 'been there and done it'. His writing is the solid teaching of a church builder and experienced disciple maker. One could easily use this text to walk a young believer through to Christian maturity and fruitfulness.

Overall, this is a really helpful book that will help you to 'walk as children of light'.

Brian Bernays, Senior Minister,
C3 Church, Tamworth, NSW, Australia.

Pastor Don's book presents us with relevant and helpful teaching "for such a time as this", pointing us back to God's directive to "be holy as I am Holy". Inspiring, challenging. A must read for all who long to enjoy the blessings of walking in the light of His Holy Presence and bringing glory to His Name through our living.

Majors Alan and Jenny Peterson (R)
The Salvation Army, Australia.

An encouraging and affirming read, helpful in the continued growing in our relationship with God through Jesus Christ, our growing in the likeness of Christ and what that means in the way we engage in the world as sincere followers of our risen Lord.

Rev. Luke Smallwood,
Uniting Church, Charters Towers, QLD, Australia.

There are only a few books that come along and joyfully call you forward to higher places in the Lord. This is such a book. While combining his passion for a radiant Christian life, through the lens of biblical holiness and church history; Don has given us a gift as a modern day spiritual father. This book is like slow release 'spiritual' fertilizer to the soul – it will nourish and equip you to be fruitful for Jesus for years to come!

Rev. Jeff Baills,
Baptist Minister, Police Chaplain, QLD, Australia.

"A Radiant Character" is therapy for the soul, filled with memorable quotes, straight talk and the big question, "Who are you and what are you doing here?" Pastor Don unpacks The Life, The Truth and The Way, encouraging the reader to thank the Lord for all of the experiences of life and the way He promised to bring good out of them.

This book is an insightful read, and excellent teaching tool, with comprehensive references and added appeal to those unable to be part of a church community. "A Radiant Character" it is a powerful message for all serious believers, administering the spiritual oxygen of the cross as we become new beings in Christ.

Min (Merilyn) Jones,
Director **Backtrack Australia,**
Past **Scripture Union** QLD Outback Regional Manager.

OTHER BOOKS: in the *You Can...* series

Go to https://cypressproject.com.au

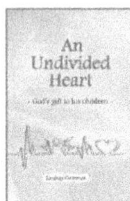

You Can Make An Impact

Don Hardgrave, 236 pages

You Can Discover God's Will

Don Hardgrave, 194 pages

OTHER BOOKS: discipleship & biblical studies

Go to https://cypressproject.com.au

An Undivided Heart

Lindsay Cameron, 214 pages

You Can Make An Impact

Lindsay Cameron, 166 pages

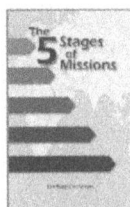

The 5 Stages of Missions

Lindsay Cameron, 158 pages

www.ingramcontent.com/pod-product-compliance
Lightning Source LLC
Chambersburg PA
CBHW060240050426
42448CB00009B/1530